World-renowned experts join those with
Asperger's Syndrome to resolve issues that
girls and women face every day!

Asperger's
and Girls

Featuring **Tony Attwood** *and*
Temple Grandin, *plus 7 more experts*

Future Horizons, Inc. • Arlington, Texas

Asperger's and Girls

World-renowned experts join those with Asperger's Syndrome to resolve issues that girls and women face every day!

All marketing and publishing rights
guaranteed to and reserved by:

FUTURE HORIZONS INC.

721 W. Abram Street
Arlington, TX 76013
Toll-free: 800-489-0727
Phone: 817-277-0727
Fax: 817-277-2270
Website: *www.FHautism.com*
E-mail: *info@FHautism.com*

ISBN 10:1-932565-40-X
ISBN 13:978-1-932565-40-9

Printed in Canada

Asperger's
and Girls

Table of Contents

Foreword

As a girl growing up with Asperger's, I had one thing in common with boys with Asperger's: I was one of those kids who "just didn't fit in." Often, no one knew quite what to do with me or how to react to my eccentricities.

What do you do with a little girl who can't play dolls with other girls because they don't do it "right"? I had read many child psychology books, including Dr. Spock's *Baby and Child Care*, so I absolutely knew how to play dolls correctly. The other girls just played any old way and weren't concerned about correct infant care.

And what do you do with a girl who gets into arguments on the playground because the typical girls don't recognize that Sabrina is the *best* of Charlie's Angels? After all, she was the "brainy" one, and smartest is best, right?

Of course, I learned about puberty very logically, hunting through the library for studies on human mating behaviors in various cultures and painstakingly dissecting tampons in my bedroom. Judy Blume was not nearly enough for me!

During the mandatory sixth-grade sex-ed talk, when I "tuned out," staring at the ceiling, the teacher let it pass, assuming that I was embarrassed by the subject matter. In reality, I refused to listen to the teacher because she had made incorrect statements about embryonic development, and I didn't want to listen to someone who was obviously ignorant.

I was, to the other girls (and a lot of the teachers), a weirdo whose behavior just couldn't be explained. Like many women, I would not have been diagnosed with Asperger's if it weren't for the diagnosis of a close family member: my brother Jimmy, who has autism. In fact, many girls and women with AS don't find out about this important neurological difference until that very difference creates a disastrous or near-disastrous situation, finally bringing (hopefully appropriate) professional attention to them.

This book is, among other things, a much-needed and much-deserved nod of recognition to all of us female humans with AS. Heaven knows we deserve it; at last, parents, teachers, and psychologists are becoming aware that we are a unique population with distinct and concrete needs.

In addition to being a small step towards bringing the distaff side of AS into the light, this book also offers much information and support for those who live, work, study, or play with girls with Asperger's.

Inside, the reader will find such gems as information from Tony Attwood on what we know—and don't know—about why it is so hard to find the girls with Asperger's who have been empirically demonstrated to exist.

Catherine Faherty talks about the problems that are unique to women with AS, and how these have been brought out via a unique support-group program at TEACCH.

Sheila Wagner's contribution is a thoughtful and thorough piece not just on the problems girls with AS experience in school, but also on the necessary scope and breadth of solutions that can save many girls from being shunted aside.

Lisa Iland gives us information from the point of view of a typical teen who not only has a brother with an autism spectrum disorder, but has also made friends with some of her female peers on the spectrum. It is one thing when we with AS decide not to be part of the teen mainstream, but it is quite another to be unable to make one's own decision to do so or not due to ignorance and confusion.

Mary Wrobel writes about the practical aspects of preparing the young girl with AS for puberty and the issues that arise as girls with AS move into womanhood.

Teresa Bolick gives advice for that tricky time of moving from girlhood to womanhood; parents inclined to be overprotective should read the chapter twice.

Ruth Snyder provides insight as to her life and direction as a woman with AS who was not given the insight and support that she needed until much later than girlhood.

Temple Grandin concludes the book with some words of wisdom on the importance of careers as well as the reasons for her lack of interest in dating.

There is also a chapter of mine in there, about issues pertaining to dating and relationships.

Just as important as the information contained herein is the message: girls with Asperger's need and deserve to get the support and education they need to be the women they can be, instead of spending their lives struggling invisibly.

We women and girls with AS are here, and we deserve to be recognized, to be supported by our families and each other, and to have lives of our own. I like to say, "We're here, we're weird, get used to it!"

Jennifer McIlwee Myers
August 2006

The Pattern of Abilities and Development of Girls with Asperger's Syndrome

Meet Tony Attwood, Ph.D.

Dr. Attwood is a clinical psychologist who lives and works in Brisbane, Australia. Over the past thirty years, he has worked with thousands of individuals with autism, Asperger's Syndrome, and Pervasive Developmental Disorder. His patients have ranged in age from infants to octogenarians, from profoundly disabled persons to university professors. He presents workshops and training courses for parents, professionals, and individuals with autism throughout the world.

His books and DVDs on Asperger's Syndrome and High-Functioning Autism are recognized as the best offerings in the field. His book, *Asperger's Syndrome: A Guide for Parents and Professionals*, has already sold over 300,000 copies, and has been translated into twenty languages. Undoubtedly, his new book, *Complete Guide to Asperger's Syndrome,* will be equally insightful.

Are females less likely than males to be born with Asperger's Syndrome (AS)—or are they simply less likely to be diagnosed? Statistics show a significant diagnostic "gender gap" when it comes to AS: for every ten boys, only one girl is diagnosed.

Like others in his field, Dr. Attwood has given much thought to this disparity. In the following article, he suggests that Asperger's girls may simply be slipping under the radar, and offers a number of fascinating reasons for why and how this can happen.

T he overwhelming majority of referrals for a diagnostic assessment for Asperger's Syndrome are boys. The ratio of males to females is around 10:1, yet the epidemiological research for Autistic Spectrum Disorders suggests that the ratio should be 4:1. Why are girls less likely to be identified as having the characteristics indicative of Asperger's Syndrome? The following are some tentative suggestions that have yet to be validated by academic research, but they provide some plausible explanations based on preliminary clinical experience.

It appears that many girls with Asperger's Syndrome have the same profile of abilities as boys, but a subtler, or less severe, expression of the characteristics. Parents may be reluctant to seek a diagnostic assessment if the child appears to be coping reasonably well, and clinicians may be hesitant to commit themselves to a diagnosis unless the signs are conspicuously different from the normal range of behavior and abilities.

We have a stereotype of typical female and male behavior. Girls are more able to verbalize their emotions and less likely to use physically aggressive acts in response to negative emotions such as confusion, frustration and anger. We do not know whether this is a cultural or constitutional characteristic, but we recognize that children who are aggressive are more likely to be referred for a diagnostic assessment to determine if the behavior is due to a specific developmental disorder, and for advice on behavior management. Hence, boys with Asperger's Syndrome are more often referred to a psychologist or psychiatrist because their aggression has become a concern for their parents or schoolteacher. A consequence of this referral bias is that not only are more boys referred, clinicians and academics can also have a false impression of the incidence of aggression in this population.

One must always consider the personality of the person with Asperger's Syndrome and how they cope with the difficulties they experience in social reasoning, empathy and cognition. Some individuals are overtly active participants in social situations. Their unusual profile of abilities in social situations is quite obvious. However, some are reluctant to socialize with others and their personalities can be described as passive. They can become quite adept at camouflaging their difficulties and clinical experience suggests that the passive personality is more common in girls.

Each person with Asperger's Syndrome develops their own techniques and strategies to acquire specific skills and develop coping mechanisms. One technique is to have practical guidance and moral support from one's peers. We know that children with Asperger's Syndrome elicit from others either strong maternal or "predatory" behavior. If the person's natural peer group is girls, they are more likely to be supported and included by a greater majority of their peers. Thus girls with Asperger's Syndrome are often "mothered" by other girls. They may prompt the child when she is unsure what to do or say in social situations and comfort her when she is distressed. In contrast, boys are notorious for their intolerance of children who are different and are more prone to be "predatory." This can have an unfortunate effect on the behavior of a boy with Asperger's Syndrome and many complain of being teased, ignored or bullied by other boys. It is interesting to note that some boys with

Asperger's Syndrome actually prefer to play with girls, who are often kinder and more tolerant than their male peers.

The author has conducted both individual and group social skills training of boys and girls with Asperger's Syndrome. Experience has indicated that, in general, the girls are more motivated to learn and quicker to understand key concepts in comparison to boys with Asperger's Syndrome of equivalent intellectual ability. Thus, they may have a better long-term prognosis in terms of becoming more fluent in their social skills. This may explain why women with Asperger's Syndrome are often less conspicuous than men with the syndrome, and therefore less likely to be referred for a diagnostic assessment. The author has also noted that, in general, mothers with Asperger's Syndrome appear to have more "maternal" and empathic abilities with their own children than fathers with Asperger's Syndrome, who can have great difficulty understanding and relating to their children.

Some individuals with Asperger's Syndrome can be quite ingenious in using imitation and modeling to camouflage their difficulties in social situations. One strategy that has been used by many girls and some boys is to observe people who are socially skilled and to copy their mannerisms, voice, and persona. This is a form of social echolalia, or mirroring, where the person acquires a superficial social competence by acting the part of another person. This is illustrated in Liane Holliday-Willey's intriguing autobiography, titled, *Pretending to be Normal*:

> *I could take part in the world as an observer. I was an avid observer. I was enthralled with the nuances of people's actions. In fact, I often found it desirable to become the other person. Not that I consciously set out to do that, rather it came as something I simply did. As if I had no choice in the matter. My mother tells me I was very good at capturing the essence and persona of people. At times I literally copied someone's looks and their actions. I was uncanny in my ability to copy accents, vocal inflections, facial expressions, hand movements, gaits and tiny gestures. It was as if I became the person I was emulating.*

Girls are more likely to be enrolled in speech and drama lessons, and this provides an ideal and socially acceptable opportunity for coaching in body language. Many people with Asperger's Syndrome have a prodigious memory and this can include reciting the dialogue for all characters in a play and memorizing the dialogue or "script" of real life conversations. Knowing the script also means the child does not have to worry about what to say. Acting can subsequently become a successful career option, although there can be some confusion when adults with Asperger's Syndrome act another persona in real life, as this can be misconstrued as Multiple Personality Disorder rather than a constructive means of coping with Asperger's Syndrome.

When a child would like more friends but clearly has little success in this area, one option is to create imaginary friends. This often occurs with young girls who visualize friends in their solitary play or use dolls as a substitute for real people. Girls with Asperger's Syndrome can create imaginary friends and elaborate doll play that superficially resembles the play of other girls, but there can be several qualitative differences. They often lack reciprocity in their natural social play and can be too controlling when playing with their peers. This is illustrated in Liane Holliday-Willey's autobiography.

> *The fun came from setting up and arranging things. Maybe this desire to organize things rather than play with things, is the reason I never had a great interest in my peers. They always wanted to use the things I had so carefully arranged. They would want to rearrange and redo. They did not let me control the environment.*

When involved with solitary play with dolls, the girl with Asperger's Syndrome has total control and can script and direct the play without interference and having to accept outcomes suggested by others. The script and actions can be an almost perfect reproduction of a real event or scene from a book or film. While the special interest in collecting and playing with dolls can be assumed to be an age-appropriate activity and not indicative of psychopathology, the dominance and intensity of the interest is unusual. Playing with and talking to imaginary friends and dolls can also continue into the teenage years, when the person would have been expected to mature beyond such play. This quality can be misinterpreted as evidence of hallucinations and delusions and a diagnostic assessment for schizophrenia rather than Asperger's Syndrome.

The most popular special interests of boys with Asperger's Syndrome are types of transport, and specialized areas of science and electronics, particularly computers. It has now become a more common reaction of clinicians to consider whether a boy with an encyclopedic knowledge in these areas has Asperger's Syndrome. Girls with Asperger's Syndrome can be interested in the same topics, but clinical experience suggests their special interest can be animals and classic literature. These interests are not typically associated with boys with Asperger's Syndrome. The interest in animals can be focused on horses or native animals and this characteristic dismissed as simply typical of young girls. However, the intensity and qualitative aspects of the interest are unusual. Teenage girls with Asperger's Syndrome can also develop a fascination with classic literature such as the plays of Shakespeare and poetry. Both have an intrinsic rhythm that they find entrancing, and some develop their writing skills and fascination with words to become successful authors, poets or academics in English literature. Some adults with Asperger's Syndrome are now examining the works of famous authors for indications of the unusual perception and reasoning associated with Asperger's Syndrome. One example is the short story "Cold" in *Elementals: Stories of Fire and Ice* by A.S. Byatt.

Finally, the author has noted that some women with Asperger's Syndrome can be unusual in their tone of voice. Their tone resembles a much younger person, having an almost childlike quality. Many are concerned about the physiological changes during puberty and prefer to maintain the characteristics of childhood. Like boys with Asperger's Syndrome, girls may see no value in being fashionable, preferring practical clothing and not using cosmetics or deodorants. This latter characteristic can be quite conspicuous.

These tentative explanations for the apparent underrepresentation of girls with Asperger's Syndrome have yet to be examined by objective research studies. It is clear that we need more epidemiological studies to establish the true incidence in girls, and for research on the clinical signs, cognitive abilities, and adaptive behavior to include an examination of any quantitative and qualitative differences between male and female subjects. In the meantime, girls with Asperger's Syndrome are likely to continue to be overlooked and not to receive the degree of understanding and resources they need.

Reference:
Holliday-Willey, L. (1999) *Pretending to be Normal: Living with Asperger's Syndrome*. London. Jessica Kingsley Publications.

Asperger's Syndrome in Women:
A Different Set of Challenges?

Meet Catherine Faherty

Catherine Faherty recognized her calling at age thirteen, when she worked with differently-abled children at a summer day camp. Since then, she has taught children and teens with autism, and now trains teachers and other professionals (locally, nationally, and internationally) in addition to consulting with parents and schools about autism. She also develops training models and manuals at the Asheville, North Carolina TEACCH Center, where she works as a psychoeducational specialist with people on the spectrum. She is the author of a workbook for children with autism and their parents and teachers: *Asperger's ... What Does it Mean to Me?*

Support groups have long proven their efficacy in helping people come to terms with specific issues. Group members share stories, problems, and solutions that benefit everyone. But what if, while you share many of the group's concerns, you are still a minority within the group? The predominance of Asperger's men in Asperger's support groups can make it difficult for Asperger's women to air problems that are unique to females.

When a young woman in her adult social group at the TEACCH Center expressed a desire for more information that focused solely on the problems facing Asperger's females, Ms. Faherty responded by forming a women's group. In the following article, she reveals the concerns that are shared by this "minority within a minority."

A young woman who has participated for several years in a social group for adults with high functioning autism and Asperger's, sponsored at our TEACCH Center in Asheville, recently remarked, "There aren't a heck of a lot of women who have Asperger's or autism. The majority are males, and although we get along with the guys, there are some issues that they are never going to understand. I wish there was more information specifically for women who have autism." Her comment prompted the initiation of the first women's group at the Asheville TEACCH Center. While talking with this woman, who is in her twenties, I was reminded of my own early adulthood. I remember the strong camaraderie and support of "women's consciousness-raising groups" that sprouted up on college campuses and in living rooms in the 60s and 70s. While struggling for and demanding equality between the sexes in the society at large, we discovered that there were important distinctions that needed to be honored. Together we explored and defined what "being a woman" was about, in the company of other young women searching for self-awareness. Being a member of a women's "CR" (Consciousness-Raising) group was educational, exciting, exhilarating, emotional, relevant—and never boring.

According to Tony Attwood and other professionals in the field, women with high functioning autism and Asperger's may be an under-diagnosed population. If this is true, some of the reasons may be attributed to gender differences.

Are there behaviors that are seen in girls with Asperger's, but not in boys, that we haven't yet identified as part of the profile, or certain gender-related behavior that might fool us into ruling out the diagnosis? What about the "pretend play" that has been observed in many young girls at our center, which on the surface appears to be quite creative and imaginative? There seem to be many girls (on the spectrum) who are enamored with princesses, fantasy kingdoms, unicorns, and animals. How many diagnosticians observe these interests and skills as imagination, and rule out a diagnosis based on these behaviors? Might this interest in imaginary kingdoms and talking animals be more common among girls than boys, yet still exist alongside other autistic/AS traits?

And what about one typical response to confusion or frustration—hitting or other such outward expressions of frustration? Does this type of acting out occur more often in boys with autism than in girls? Is confusion or frustration simply easier to identify in boys than girls because we already look for it? Among the general population, it is commonly thought that boys do "act out" more than girls. (You sometimes hear a teacher complain there are too many boys in his or her class, and about its impact on the class's personality!) Is it easier to identify boys as having autism because their behaviors are more obvious than those of girls who may experience inward or passive signs of aggression?

Professionals whose task it is to diagnose individuals with autism or Asperger's need to learn more about the full range of qualities and personality differences unique to girls and women on the spectrum.

And what about the girls' and women's route to self-understanding? Indeed, several women I have worked with who have Asperger's have talked about the unique challenges they experience because they constitute a "minority" within this special group of society.

I believe that in order to gain self-understanding, each person with—or without—autism needs to see his or her own reflection in the world. I call this "seeing one's place." For people with autism or AS, who are already challenged in this area, it becomes imperative that they meet, listen to, talk with, read about, and learn from others with autism. What happens as a result of this coming together is that they are able to see their "reflection" and better understand their own unique styles of thinking and being. Women with autism, although benefiting greatly from getting to know other people with autism, often find that they are the only woman (or one of very few women) in the group.

When I asked the women we see at our center if they would be interested in being in a women's group, I had hoped that the group could fill a gap in our services. I also hoped that I would learn more about what it means to be a woman with autism. The more I meet with these women, the more I realize we have far to go in understanding the unique challenges that women with autism or Asperger's face.

One woman explained that, from her perspective, there is subtle interaction between two sets of issues. "Problems related to the [autism] spectrum are combined with problems of society's expectations of women. How one looks, what one wears, how one is supposed to relate socially, that a woman is supposed to have a natural empathy towards others, expectations about dating and marriage…." Women are affected by autism in the same ways as their male counterparts; however, they are doubly challenged by the added assumptions that society places on the female gender.

At the risk of stereotyping, any man who is a rational thinker and not emotionally in tune with others is often thought of as having "typical male behavior" (think of the TV show *Home Improvement*). A woman exhibiting these same personality traits might be regarded as odd, annoying, cold, or, depending on the situation, even mean-spirited. Autism, with its particular effects on personality, causes one to appear more rational and less emotionally responsive or empathetic to others. Women with autism note that these expectations indeed may weigh more heavily on them, just because they are women.

At the first meeting, the group members requested specific topics for discussion, issues that they encounter in daily life or ones that they are currently pondering. These included issues that are relevant to women at large such as personal safety; dating and sex; or being taken advantage of when your car needs repair. Other issues they raised were felt by group members to possibly be more significant for women with autism, but common to all—being pressured to conform by getting married; to "act like a lady"; and issues about one's appearance—to have to "look a certain way."

However, there were topics that all agree are a direct result of being a woman with autism, such as common behavioral and social expectations by the society at large. At the top of the list were the expectations of being sensitive to others and displaying empathy.

Women with autism have expressed their feeling that more is expected from them than from their male counterparts, simply because of their gender. Members of the group felt that expectations to be sensitive and empathetic—qualities typically attributed to women—are unfair and difficult to meet. Discussion centered on how these behaviors require skills such as the ability to accurately read and respond to body language, along with the inherent desire to "take care of others, emotionally." Interestingly, after discussing these issues, the first requested topic was how to read body language and how to tell if someone is trying to take advantage of you.

The topic that generated the strongest emotional response from the group was the members' personal experience of feeling as though they were being treated like children. Parents are often more protective of their daughters than their sons. Daughters with autism talked about feeling overly protected into womanhood. In many cases, this is needed, although without understanding the parent's perspective, the adult daughter can feel unfairly babied. Some women talked about the resentment they felt toward people who for many years had been trying to teach them "socially appropriate" ways of acting. "Enough already!" was a common response.

The desire to be respected as an individual, and as a woman, was voiced clearly and strongly. Although it is probable that men with autism wish just as fervently to be respected as individuals and as men, it was the women who voiced these desires clearly, with deep emotion and passion, when talking with other women.

A personal note from Catherine Faherty:

I want to thank the members of this first group who have given me permission to share this information. For those of us who live and work with women with autism, it unveils a new perspective on how we must think about and relate to the disability. I applaud and encourage other women with autism—and those who care about them—to form women's groups for support, encouragement, and, in the words of one group member, "…understanding from like-minded peers."

Educating the Female Student with Asperger's

Meet Sheila Wagner, M.Ed.

S heila Wagner has twenty years experience in the field of autism, and has written *Inclusive Programming for Elementary Students with Autism*, which won the Autism Society of America's Literary Award for 2000; *Inclusive Programming for Middle School Students with Autism/Asperger's Syndrome*; and is co-author of *Understanding Asperger's Syndrome FAST FACTS*. Her *Inclusive Programming* books each provide an inclusion program for students with severe disabilities. (Keep your eye out for her next book, *Inclusive Programming for High School Students with Autism*.) Her engaging and readable style, coupled with her extensive knowledge and classroom practice, makes her books indispensable to professionals and nonprofessionals alike.

This article explores why the system fails to diagnose Asperger's girls, and asks, "Are we as a nation setting standards for educating students with AS based solely on boys?" The answer: "Yes." Sheila Wagner proposes solutions so practical you'll wonder why they weren't implemented long before: better training at all academic levels; peer programs enlisting fellow students to integrate AS girls into the school community; social-skills groups comprised of girls instead of groups populated primarily by boys; modified academic strategies and girls-only instruction on menstruation and sexual issues. Equally valuable is a list of behaviors to alert teachers that a girl should be evaluated for Asperger's. This list should be in every educator's office, and would go far toward answering the poignant question, "Where are the female students with Asperger's Syndrome?"

"I want you to come and observe a girl in my class. Something is very odd, and I don't know how to help her. She says the most outrageous things in the middle of a lesson, disrupting the class. The other students will have nothing to do with her, and because of her odd behaviors, she has no friends at all." This would be worrisome if it was elementary school, but this is high school—the sophomore year. This student, "Cary," is small for her age and is very bright, but struggles in almost all classes. She scurries down the hallway between class segments and doesn't talk to a soul. She trails a small, overnight suitcase on wheels that bumps into students in the crowded hall (she does not seem to notice), generating frowns and angry looks from those around her. Upon entering her next classroom, Cary immediately goes to the teacher and tells her that she was up very late the previous night doing her homework for this class, and her mother told her to go to bed. She was not able to complete the assignment and she blames her mother. She then goes over and sits at her desk, shuffles through the myriad papers crumpled in her suitcase, and pulls out a blank paper, a book, and a broken pencil. Cary does not talk to any of the other students coming into the class, nor do they talk to her, even though all the other students are talking and laughing together. During class time (English lit—a discussion of Shakespeare and *Othello*), Cary is very attentive and wants to answer all the questions and is interested in the lesson, offering her analysis of the dialogue, firmly believing that she understands the motivation and thoughts of the characters. She blurts out time and again, needing reminders to raise her hand. When she is called on, Cary provides such extensive detail about the conversations taking place in the text that the teacher must interrupt to move on with the lesson. Unfortunately, her interpretation of this complex text is simplistic, often missing the meaning of the intense dialogue between characters, resulting in peers glancing her way and rolling their eyes—all of which she misses. Despite her high participation in this class, she is only earning a C-, due to her difficulties with the content, her tardiness with assignments, and the borderline quality of her written work. She also does not participate well in group projects because she insists on directing the scope of the assignment, eliminating another valued grade. Her parents are worried for her and do not know what her future will hold, since she does not appear to have any long-term goals or strong motivation about her future.

What is the problem here? Maybe a better question is: *where do we start in listing them?* Although this student went on to receive a diagnosis of Asperger's Syndrome, the question that begs to be answered is, "Why did it take so long?" This student is in high school, not elementary school.

Identification of students with Asperger's Syndrome is still difficult in our nation's schools, but is improving somewhat as a result of numerous publications on Asperger's Syndrome, a selection of which includes Attwood, T., 1998; Myles, B. S. & Adreon 2001; Myles & Southwick 2005; Myles & Simpson, 2003; Bashe, Kirby, Cohen & Attwood, 2005; Willey, 1999; Jackson & Attwood, 2002; Wagner, 2004, leading to better teacher training and knowledge of this disorder. Still, Asperger's Syndrome continues to be the stepchild of the Autism Spectrum Disorders. Because of the somewhat heightened recognition, many male students with Asperger's are identified early, but the same cannot be claimed for the females in this population. When considering the entire spectrum of students with autism disorders, the ratio of males-to-females diagnosed is 4 to 1(Ehlers and Gillberg, 1993), but as cognitive abilities rise, the ratio of male/female also rises with Asperger's Syndrome showing a 10:1 ratio in *clinical* settings (Attwood, 1999). Amazingly, referrals for evaluation and diagnosis of boys are almost ten times higher than for girls (Gillberg, 1989), causing us to better examine the reasons for this disparity. In considering these statistics, we must ask: *where are the female students with Asperger's Syndrome?* Once found, what are the different considerations that must be noted diagnostically and, ultimately, educationally, when developing programs for girls as opposed to boys with this disorder? It begs the question: *are we as a nation setting standards for educating students with AS based solely on boys?* How are the girls surviving through the educational years? It is, perhaps, time to take a more critical look at this population in schools, in order to better define the similarities and differences of boys versus girls with Asperger's disorder and thus better the chances of support and integration.

The case scenario outlined above is typical of female students with Asperger's Syndrome. "Cary" has made it through to high school without identification, appropriate support or trained teachers. She has most likely been met with social isolation, lowered grades, loneliness, confusion and, as with so many with this disorder, depression. Her teachers have passed her through the years because she is bright and has managed grades above failing, even though she appears to be so different from the other students and is not living up to her documented intelligence scores. If we could go back in time with current training and knowledge, we might have a better chance at catching this student and providing the help she requires to reach her full potential. So let us try to prevent this same outcome for other female students who are suspected of having Asperger's Syndrome.

The Role of Training

School Psychologists
It is critical for the nation's school systems to be, first and foremost, trained in the area of Asperger's Syndrome in order to recognize this disability in their student population. Many, if not most, school psychologists obtain training in the area of autism, though the breadth and depth of that training can vary widely from school to school, and state to state. Ultimately, special education directors and administrators are looking to

school psychologists to help them sort out the various disabilities. School psychologists need to stay ahead of the game by being fully knowledgeable of the upper regions of the Autism spectrum and Asperger's Syndrome in specific. Without this specialized training, the very people who should clarify the disorder will likely be the ones who will send this student down the wrong educational road, attributing the difficulties faced by Asperger's students to the more emotionally-laden disabilities, to learning disorders, or to attention-deficit/hyperactivity disorder. Asperger's is different, and so much more.

Catherine Faherty (2002) suggests that "it is easier to identify boys as having autism because [their] behaviors are more obvious than girls who may experience inward or passive signs of aggression." Because of this milder presentation, many females with Asperger's may go undiagnosed. School psychologists must recognize that the female student with AS will pose a somewhat different profile than the boys with this disorder. This fact must be imbedded within any training on Asperger's Syndrome. Many characteristics will be the same, of course, since the diagnostic criteria for Asperger's Syndrome in the *Diagnostic and Statistical Manual–IV-TR* (American Psychiatric Association, 2000) do not differentiate between boys and girls. However, this author will highlight some clinical and anecdotal points that have been observed over the years in the hopes of diagnosing the girls with this syndrome sooner, and providing them with better educational programs. The following are some points to ponder.

- Girls with AS are often missed in the early elementary years because they may be viewed more as passive personalities, rather than as girls with social impairments.

- Girls with AS may not call attention to themselves as boys with AS often do by posing a disruption factor to the classroom.

- Girls with AS may also show perseverative interests (such as Barbie dolls, Bratz Girls, unicorns, horses, and ponies), but they may simply appear to be age-typical. It is not at all unusual for little girls to be "horse-crazy" and carry it throughout their lives, but typical girls who are "horse-crazy" are usually able to expand their areas of interest and be captured by other activities as well, especially new fads that seem to come down the pike with regularity; the female with Asperger's Syndrome may not.

- Many boys with AS struggle with math; girls with AS may also struggle with math, but their difficulties may be dismissed because "girls don't do well in math anyway."

- Girls with AS who have difficulty making sustained eye contact with others are often viewed as shy, coy, embarrassed, or naïve and innocent, rather than as having the poor social skills inherent in an autism spectrum disorder.

Handwriting difficulties may be one area that can be picked up as an early indicator that separates them from their female peers. Typical female students in elementary school usually love to color, to stay in the lines and to draw detailed pictures of horses and families. The female student with AS may hate drawing and coloring and do poorly at it. When boys with AS color, they sometimes hate it, too, though it is often dismissed because all boys tend to use larger strokes, lose interest in adhering to the strict guidelines of coloring within the lines, and couldn't care less if their marks go astray (though this is a broad generalization, of course).

Girls with AS will face the same difficulties in the social domain that boys with AS face, but the difficulties may not be recognized as such and their profiles may appear more mild. Hints as to the true diagnosis can be found by teachers and psychologists who watch for the discrepancy between typical girls' social maturation and that of girls with AS. Typical girls become socially savvy early—choosing "boyfriends," becoming enamored of the latest fashions, having early knowledge, and sometimes use, of make-up, of the latest fads in clothes and fashion, and are very cognizant of what other girls are doing in this social realm—even in early elementary grades. Typical girls are interested in how they are viewed by their peers and by the opposite sex far earlier than the boys are. Girls with Asperger's are lost in this area, being much more socially immature and reticent than their typical age-mates. If this were the only area of difficulty, they might indeed be just socially immature. But their female counterparts in school leave girls who have AS in the social dust quite quickly.

Although girls with AS fall behind their female age-mates early in their social/peer relationships, this area may not be recognized as part of a disability simply because of the ways in which society views females (Faherty, 2002). Women are assumed to take a more subservient or withdrawn role in comparison to the rough-and-tumble boys, and if one girl is much more hesitant to take part in the whirlwind of age-related social culture, many parents thank their lucky stars, and teachers are delighted with their "innocence" and view them as "sweet." After all, most parents are truly horrified when they finally understand the words to popular music and are shocked at the actions taking place in video games or movies. Who wouldn't be grateful if their little girl did not seem interested in them? What is wrong with that? By itself, of course, nothing; when counted as a component of, and in combination with other areas of difficulty, worrisome.

School psychologists above all should be knowledgeable enough to at least question the presence of Asperger's Syndrome in female students who are referred to them. Any time there is the combination of social immaturity, perseverative interests, lack of eye contact, poor handwriting, poor gross motor coordination, repetitive behaviors, isolation or teasing by peers, falling grades, and being viewed as "odd" by teachers and peers, Asperger's Syndrome should be investigated.

Teachers

Although we always wish that the teachers would have sufficient knowledge and training in the entire spectrum of autism, this is rarely the case, especially when taking the general education teachers into account in an inclusive classroom. The results of a recent study (Mandell, et al., 2005) clarified the average age for those already diagnosed with Asperger's Syndrome to be 7.1 years for males and 7.3 years in females due to limited knowledge in the presentation of the disorder, prognosis and treatment of ASD, and the suspicion of other developmental disorders delaying the referral for evaluation. So it is not uncommon for teachers to be among the first group of people that picks up inconsistencies in behavior or performance with a particular student. Teachers are in a unique position to compare one student to a whole host of typical students and clarify where someone is diverging from the developmental pathway generally walked by most students. This is a perspective that parents, with the exception of comparing their child to siblings or cousins, do not have. Teachers see it all, but if not cognizant of this sophisticated developmental disorder, may not pick up the signs early enough to refer them for an evaluation or to make changes in educational programs sufficient to produce improvement.

Once the disorder is recognized, training should be offered to *all* of the student's teachers. This becomes imperative as the student ages and travels through the system, since research has shown that treatment yields diminishing returns with older students (Mars, Mauk & Dowrick, 1998). Ideally, if we wish for this girl to show improvement in needed skills, it will come as a result of encountering multitudes of trained teachers as she ages. In elementary school, the teachers she will encounter include the special education teacher, general education teacher, teachers for P.E., art and music, as well as support and related staff. However, as middle school and high school come onto the horizon, the number of teachers involved with this same student will rise dramatically. You now have a team of teachers for general education classes alone, plus the special education teacher, and any teachers of elective classes that are chosen each term. The difficult part is that, at end of term, all those teachers may change and another whole set of teachers needing training will begin teaching her. All students with disabilities, including the female student with AS, deserve to have teachers who are knowledgeable in their disorder so that students receive the most appropriate education, but this business of training keeps getting more intense over the years. It is a critical need that is often not met, resulting in the lack of diagnosis, fewer students being recognized under appropriate educational eligibility, and less effective teaching strategies being employed in the classroom, generating socially-isolated, lonely, potentially depressed individuals who will not be able to capitalize on their high potential.

Educational Programs for the Female Student with AS

Peer Programming and Support

As with male students with Asperger's Syndrome, the female student with Asperger's will need the help and support of her typical peer classmates in order to improve her skills, and to increase the opportunities for a better outcome. Research has clearly proven that peer programming can help students with disabilities become better-included in the typical population at schools (Strain, Shores, & Timm, 1977; Odom, Hoyson, Jamieson, & Strain, 1985; Roeyers, H., 1996; Kamps, D. M., Barbetta, P. M., & Delquadri, J, 1994 among so many other researchers). Peer programming is a tried-and-true means to overcome the huge barriers posed in the areas of academics and the social and behavioral interactions that students struggle with on a day-to-day basis. It also targets a critical area of instruction that is difficult for a teacher to address. In light of the female student with Asperger's, we need to look closely at this area of peer support and recognize that the area our special needs student struggles in is the very same area that typical students fight over to gain dominance. Typical girls mature more rapidly than their male counterparts and learn how to use sophisticated levels of verbal and non-verbal communication too quickly, isolating non-favored girls from a group. Cliques form rapidly and change often—sometimes within the span of a day. A collection of three boys is not usually a problem; a collection of three girls is almost always a problem. This mastery of the verbal and non-verbal communication by typical girls often results in the girl with Asperger's being quickly targeted for exclusion, and it is highly likely that she will remain isolated unless peer programming can be established in the classroom and fostered throughout the school.

Peer programming will take on different structures depending on the age and grade of the students. In elementary school, the whole-class approach can be quite formal, with the individual's accomplishments helping the entire class earn rewards for helping one another. In middle school, it is often wiser to begin with a small group of socially mature, trustworthy students to build a core network of peers with the expectation that they will not only support her in class, but also protect her in hallways and the lunchroom, and help to deflect the (sometimes vicious) teasing and bullying she may encounter. In high school, individual students can be found to support this young woman in elective classes, after-school activities and from the college-track and socially or community-aware organizations such as Beta Club, Honor's Club, Environmental Club, etc.

Regardless of what age this student with Asperger's is, teachers and parents should investigate and implement peer programming in order to build socially appropriate behaviors, improve chances of acceptance, better the possibility of inclusion, increase self-esteem and lessen the chances of depression. This student should go through the educational years with *all* her areas of need addressed, not forgetting the important skills of social interaction and how their mastery will impact her entire life.

Academic Modifications

Girls with Asperger's Syndrome will face the same academic challenges as boys, but may not be as vocal about their struggles, nor call the teacher's attention to them as readily as the boys will. In this author's experience, girls with Asperger's are much more likely to suffer in silence, hoping that they won't cause the teacher to become upset with them, and many times they try desperately to hide their difficulties. As they age and the class content becomes more abstract, calling for higher order thinking, we in this business of inclusion often see these students withdraw into themselves, and sometimes demonstrate an increased anxiety regarding assignments. It is likely that this student will disappear into the mix of students who just barely get by with passing grades and are viewed as poor performers. Expectations for this student begin to lower over the years until teachers anticipate that she will not likely succeed in post-secondary institutions, and start lining her up for lower-paying jobs as an outcome. This is unfortunate. Because, with academic modifications, many female students with Asperger's could very likely go on to college, university, or a technical school, and pursue a professional job. But what academic modifications would prove helpful?

Academic modifications for this student could include:
Pre-teaching of content: Typical girls are sometimes hesitant to raise their hand in class if they do not understand the content and want to avoid being looked on as "stupid" or "dumb" by the peers. Girls with Asperger's may feel the same hesitancy, but this can be eliminated if they have some advance knowledge of the content, have a better understanding of the lesson, and feel more confident of their answers. This would also be a good way to have them "shine" in the classroom and be viewed as "smart" by their peers and teachers alike. Pre-teaching can accomplish this. Alternately, if this girl is one who raises her hand to answer every question whether she knows the answer or not, pre-teaching would at least help her to know the correct answer, eliminating the negative impressions of peers

when she provides inaccurate or inappropriate responses. Pre-teaching is a great benefit to anyone with Asperger's, since it allows them to not only know the academic content and understand it at a slower pace, but can also help them make inroads into the peer population, resulting in their being viewed in a better light.

Reduced homework assignments: Almost all students with Asperger's struggle with the huge amount of homework that is assigned each night. The boys with this disorder frequently end up shutting down, having emotional storms and/or refusing to do the work; girls sometimes similarly dissolve into emotional storms including tears, shutting down and refusing to do the work. Teachers should inquire as to how much time is spent doing homework each night for these students and lessen the amount, if needed. Many families that have children with Asperger's find their entire home life is being ruled by homework, leaving little time for family time or social outings. Homework should not be destroying family lives at all. Alternatives to homework can be considered, including providing time at school to do the homework under supervision, oral testing of content, eliminating portions of the written assignments with multiple-choice answers, switching to word processing or computer generated output, etc. Homework problems appear to be at the root of school failure for many students with Asperger's—both boys and girls—and both teachers and parents should be aware of this minefield of troubles when working with someone with this disorder.

Written production: As stated above, written assignments may need analysis to try to prevent some of the common problems that we see in students with Asperger's. However, it is not wise to eliminate all aspects of writing unless there are no other choices. As an adult, this person will continue to need to write for various reasons—filling in job applications, writing letters, signing checks and paying bills, etc., although, admittedly, these needs are lessening as computers become more and more embedded into our culture. Many teachers struggle mightily to have the student with Asperger's write in cursive, creating problems where there were none before. With the exception of signing their name, adults can get by quite easily using only the printed format. Students with Asperger's often have difficulty switching from printing to cursive. This should be considered a non-issue and the student should be allowed to continue to print her letters if, after sufficient amount of practice time, she is still unable to write in cursive. Unfortunately, in this author's experience, there are teachers who press this issue beyond the student's endurance, creating far more problems than justified. It is hoped that these teachers will finally understand this disorder and cease pressing the student with AS over the writing component. Many assignments can instead be written on the computer, immediately solving the crisis. Computer skills can also open many doors for future employment.

Using perseverative interests to teach: If the student is into Barbie dolls, Bratz Girls, horses or ponies, these interests can be used to help her learn academic content. She will be much more inclined to listen to a lesson if it involves her areas of intense interest. For example, the teacher can ask her to write one paragraph on unicorns, making sure she states her topic clearly, has a beginning, middle and ending, or ask her to do a research paper on the history of horseracing.

Additional time for testing: Many of those with Asperger's Syndrome do better on tests if they have additional time. This can be accomplished in small groups away from the classroom or during study skills classes, or before/after school. Providing additional time for tests usually means that it is away from the noise and distractions of the main classroom, as well, making it easier to concentrate.

Social Skills Assessment and Intervention

Another area that needs to be addressed concerning the female student with Asperger's is the assessment of and direct instruction in social skills. Prior to helping this young woman improve her social skills, teachers and parents should have some idea of how much she diverges from the typical social pathways. Parents and teachers often have differing viewpoints as to which skills are most needed. Parents may believe that her table manners are fine, needing only a few reminders to use her napkin or fork appropriately, etc., but teachers judge how she performs independently in a loud, noisy cafeteria with hundreds of students. They may feel that her inappropriate table manners alienate peers, causing her to lose friends. Therefore, a formal assessment of social skills should be conducted prior to making the decision as to what skills should be included in any direct instructional program.

Parents and teachers should be able to select from a variety of commercially available social skills assessment instruments, including:

Social Skills Rating Scale, Gresham (AGS)

Walker-McConnell Scales of Social Competence and School Adjustment (Wadsworth/Thompson Learning)

Skillstreaming (Research Press)

These instruments have the advantage of assessing a large number of social issues and have separate forms for elementary and adolescent age ranges. One (Gresham's) includes a student self-report, which can come in handy when teaching social skills and gaining a better understanding of how the student feels they are performing. Other instruments measure social skills embedded into the wider instrument, such as the *Vineland Adaptive Behavior Scales* and the *ABAS,* but these instruments cover a smaller portion of the social skill set than the ones listed above.

When teaching social skills, direct instruction is often necessary to properly dissect individual skills, explain replacement behaviors and practice the new skill through role-playing and self-analysis, and to better explain this rather sophisticated area to those with Asperger's.

One of the difficulties encountered when teaching a female with Asperger's Syndrome is that, too often, the social skills groups conducted in schools are primarily made up of boys. The ratio of males to females diagnosed with Asperger's means that it will be easier to find a collection of boys to participate in a group and the girls will end up being overwhelmed by the male viewpoint on social skills, and have no female model. Having girls as partners in this process can be better for the female student with Asperger's. Facial expression, gesture use, vocal tone, and listening skills are different when demonstrated by boys, as opposed to girls. If no other girl is in the group to practice with, it will be more difficult for the girl to gain the correct nuances of sophisticated social skills. If teachers have identified only one girl and a number of boys to conduct a social skills group, then teachers and parents should discuss whether this would be appropriate for the one girl, how it would impact her learning of the needed skills, and make a decision whether to keep this a small group, or to form another small group composed of typical female peers. Adding typical role models to the group is always a must for any social skills groups anyway, though it is often the component most readily eliminated in schools for one reason or another. Teachers are encouraged to find the best models available within the typical peer population and invite them into the group to assist with teaching social skills to this student with Asperger's.

Social/Sexual Issues, the School Environments, and Females with AS

Social skills intervention is essential for either gender with Asperger's Syndrome, but can and should be tailored specifically for the female, especially prior to the onset of her periods. The parental role at this time is extremely important, since the young woman with Asperger's may not fully understand or appreciate what is happening to her body. She will need specific and concrete information as to the changes taking place so she is not taken by surprise and does not become frightened or upset. This area concerns schools and teachers as well, since she will be spending more than six hours a day in this setting. Teachers should work in collaboration with the parents to discuss these issues:

- Independence in managing her own menstruation needs at school
- Discreetly carrying supplies
- How and when to quietly ask permission to leave class, if needed
- What to do and whom to ask if emergencies happen and no pads are available
- Which teachers she can approach for help
- Where extra supplies are kept at school
- Gaining permission to call home to get supplies or clothing when needed
- How to handle the added emotionalism that occurs each month.

Information on each of these topics should be kept extremely concrete and basic, so that there is no room for misinterpretation. Many girls with Asperger's Syndrome make statements regarding their periods to open classrooms full of students, embarrassing their peers and teachers. They are usually unaware of how sensitive this issue is, and how public statements about their periods can immediately eliminate the possibility of friendships. Prior training by parents in collaboration with teachers can eliminate a whole host of uncomfortable and embarrassing situations for this young woman with Asperger's Syndrome.

Another problematic area in the social/sexual domain that should be discussed by parents and teachers is health instruction. Most schools in the nation have some form of sex education taught by a variety of teachers, including the counselor, health teacher, P.E. teacher, assistant principal, etc. Parents should ask to preview this curriculum and decide whether or not their daughter should have the instruction with the whole group, or have it presented in a small group or individually. Typical students alone are usually self-conscious, embarrassed or highly amused at the instruction provided and if they ask questions, they often do so to gain a reaction from their peers, to make a joke, or at least review the question in their minds a bit to make sure that they won't make a fool of themselves when asking their question. Those with Asperger's may have legitimate questions and really want the information, but may ask questions that place them in poor standing with the peers. They may misinterpret the content and ask a question that is so basic that all the other students already know it and are amazed that she does not. Because children in this society have so much exposure to sexually-explicit language, images and themes, the sex ed curricula available to schools in this day and age have adjusted to the level of basic knowledge in the population. They assume prior knowledge exists and start farther down the track with the information than our students with Asperger's find themselves. One young woman with Asperger's became very upset when the lesson discussed sexually transmitted diseases (STDs) and how a rash can be an early sign. She knew she had contact dermatitis on her arm resulting in a rash, so drew the very logical assumption that she had an STD and became very upset, crying and yelling out that she had an STD. As you can imagine, this incident had long-lasting effects amongst her peers. The wise parent and teacher will collaborate and discuss how best to deliver the content in this area to the student (whether in the classroom with all students, in a small group, or individually) so that she understands how to appropriately accept what is happening to her body and eliminate problem situations.

The last area in the social/sexual realm for parents and teachers to consider and discuss is in the perception and reality of vulnerability. Many parents are frightened about what will happen to their "little girl" in school once she enters puberty. Some parents go to the extreme of home-schooling their daughter because they know that she is highly susceptible to outside influences and suggestions, and feel that she is better off away from the middle/high school environment. Many parents are extremely protective of their daughters, where they may possibly not be as concerned for their sons. But vulnerability for both genders is very real for those with Asperger's because they lag behind their typical age-mates in knowing how to handle overtures from the opposite sex. But it would be a travesty if teachers did not address this issue to ensure that both boys and girls with Asperger's are safe in the school environment. Parents have been known to place their daughter with AS on birth control pills simply because they cannot assume she will always be safe, and they cannot always be around to protect her. This is obviously a parental decision, but teachers must assume that they need to teach safety issues to this budding young woman with Asperger's in any case. She needs to be taught personal space issues, where to touch others, where not to touch others, whom she can trust, who can touch her body (doctors, nurses), who cannot touch parts of her body, how to say "no" when receiving uncomfortable suggestions or being asked to do something she feels is wrong, etc.

The inherent social impairment in Asperger's makes those with this disorder more vulnerable to people who do not have the best intentions, but young women can and should be taught skills to protect themselves while in school and the community, and learn routines that can be used throughout their lives. It is extremely important not to express negative opinions or to induce fear in the area of sexuality, since it is a natural, biological aspect of the human condition. Many of our individuals with this disorder do go on to marry and have children of their own. How this subject is approached will set the standard for future years of happiness or unhappiness.

Much of what the author has reviewed in these few pages can apply to both boys and girls with Asperger's; but the female with Asperger's

Syndrome still has specialized needs—diagnostically and educationally—that should be recognized by parents and educators so they may better prepare her for integration into society. Much of what we already know regarding girls with Asperger's Syndrome is from experience and clinical presentations, though it is clear that this is an area ripe for solid research that will better define this subset of Asperger's. Females with Asperger's Syndrome deserve appropriate educational programs in schools and better transition planning for their future.

References:

Attwood, T. (1998). *Asperger's Syndrome: A guide for parents and professionals.* London: Jessica Kingsley.

Attwood, T. (1999). *Asperger Syndrome and Girls: The pattern of abilities and development of girls with Asperger's syndrome.* Gladstone Area: *www.fortunecity.com/meltingpot/barclay/64/id26.htm* Sept.

Bashe, P. R., Kirby, B., Cohen, S. B., & Attwood, T. (2005). *The OASIS Guide to Asperger Syndrome: Completely revised and updated: Advice, support and inspiration.* NY, NY: Crown.

Diagnostic and Statistical Manual (DSM), IV-TR (2000). Washington, DC: *American Psychiatric Association.*

Faherty, C. (2002). Asperger's Syndrome in Women: A Different Set of Challenges? *Autism-Asperger's Digest.* Arlington, TX: Future Horizons.

Harrison, P. & Oakland, T., (2003). *Adaptive Behavior Assessment System – Second Edition (ABAS-II).* San Antonio, TX: Harcourt.

Jackson, L. & Attwood, T. (2002). *Freaks, Geeks and Asperger's Syndrome: A user guide to adolescence.* Philadelphia, PN: Jessica Kingsley.

Kamps, D. M., Barbetta, P. M., & Delquadri, J, (1994). Classwide peer tutoring: An integration strategy to improve reading skills and promote peer interactions among students with autism and general education peers. *Journal of Applied Behavior Analysis.* 27, 49-61.

Mandell DS, Mayali MN, Zubritsky CD. Factors associated with diagnosis among children with autism spectrum disorders. *Pediatrics;* Dec 2005: 116, 6; Research Library pg. 1480.

Mars AE, Mauk JE, Dowrick PW. Symptoms of pervasive developmental disorders as observed in prediagnostic home videos of infants and toddlers. *J Pediatrics.* 1998; 132: 500-504

McGinnis, E., & Goldstein, A.P., (1997). Skillstreaming the elementary school child: New strategies and perspectives for teaching prosocial skills. Champaign, IL: Research Press.

Myles, B. S., (2005). *Children and youth with Asperger's syndrome: Strategies for success in inclusive settings.* Thousand Oaks, CA: Corwin Press as a subsidiary of Sage Pub.

Myles, B. S., & Simpson, R. L. (2003). *Asperger's syndrome: A guide for parents and educators.* Austin, TX: Pro-Ed.

Myles, B. S., & Southwick, J. (2005). Asperger syndrome and difficult moments: Practical solutions for tantrums, rage and meltdown. *Autism Asperger Publishing Corporation,* Shawnee Mission:KS

Odom, S. L., Hoyson, M., Jamieson, B., & Strain, P. S. (1985). Increasing handicapped preschoolers peer social interactions: Cross-setting and component analysis. *Journal of Applied Behavior Analysis, 18,* 3-16.

Sparrow, S. S., Balla, D. A., Cicchetti, D. (2005). *Vineland Adaptive Behavior Scales.* Bloomington, MN: Pearson.

Strain, P.S., Shores, R. E., & Timm, M.A., (1977). Effects of peers' social initiations on the behavior of withdrawn preschool children. *Journal of Applied Behavior Analysis, 10,* 188-198.

Walker, H.M., & McConnell, S. R. (1995). *Walker-McConnell scales of social competence and school adjustment.* Belmont, CA: Wadsworth/Thompson Learning.

Willey, L. H., (2002). *Pretending to be Normal.* Philadelphia, PA: Jessica Kingsley.

Girl to Girl:
Advice on Friendship, Bullying, and Fitting In

Meet Lisa Iland

When Lisa attended high school with her older brother Tom (who has Asperger's/HFA), she recognized that he needed help with social skills. So at age sixteen, she began writing a book about the unspoken rules that comprise the teen social code. Today she is a consultant on social skills and other teen issues for ASD teens and their families. She also presents workshops on sibling issues at conferences.

Lisa attends the highly ranked University of Redlands in Southern California, where she double-majors in Communicative Disorders and Spanish. She plans to become a bilingual Speech/Language Pathologist, specializing in social skills intervention and autism. She also enjoys singing, ballroom dancing, travel, and spending time with her family and friends.

However long it's been since you were in high school, get ready to be sucked into a time-warp. Lisa Iland recreates (and clarifies) the Byzantine world of "the rules" teenage girls live by, and which are unintelligible to Asperger's girls (not to mention the rest of us).

Her article is packed with practical advice on dealing with the "popularity hierarchy" and "levels of relationship"; how to make yourself likeable; using MTV to your advantage; combating bullies; the positive role of gossip; and more. Lisa didn't make the rules, but she doesn't pull any punches in telling you what they are.

I care about teenagers with Asperger's Syndrome because I am friends with girls on the spectrum. I empathize with the difficulties that girls with AS face, and share the joy in their social successes. My brother is also on the spectrum. When we attended high school together, I helped him problem-solve and understand the unspoken teen social rules and expectations of our peers in order to help him be successful. Although I am a typical girl, I can relate with every girl's struggle for social acceptance, but with an insider's view into the specific troubles that AS brings for high school and junior high social success. As a peer, I hope to explain the teen scene that a parent or professional may need to know about to help their child or client be successful, with rules that a teen girl with AS could use herself. Social skills attained in teen years are essential life skills for college and workplace success. I truly hope that girls with Asperger's Syndrome will find this information helpful in their daily interactions.

In forming my ideas, I interviewed two teen girls with AS on their social experiences throughout high school and junior high. I also asked dozens of my typical girl friends and classmates from high school for advice on bullying and mean girls—a school struggle for many girls with AS.

Being a typical girl, I know what most teen girls expect in friendships with other teen girls. Because girls with AS are a minority, they most likely will be forming female friendships with typical peers. I have some insight and advice for girls on the spectrum that I have formed, keeping what I have experienced are the social difficulties of AS in mind. Here are the four essential areas to know in order to fit in and find social success.

The 4 Essential Areas to Know In Order to Fit In:

- Creating Appeal and Image
- Understanding Where to Fit In
- Meeting Social Expectations
- Overcoming Bullying and Mean Girls

1. Creating Appeal and Image

There is something to like about everyone, but some people are better at being aware of and projecting their likeable traits in social situations than others. In order to make friends it is important to understand what the positive traits a girl with AS has to offer, and also what negative traits would put acceptance at risk. In order to make friends, a girl needs to be as appealing as possible and be aware of what detracts from her appeal.

From the peer perspective, I would be looking for a friend whose temperament is positive, friendly, kind, and whose actions are moderate. This would be a person who goes along with the flow of conversation, whose energy level is not overbearing, and whose volume of speech is appropriate for the setting. Overall, this girl is a nice addition to the existing social group. Things that turn friends away initially are clinginess, obnoxious hyperactivity, insults, and being overly opinionated. Once a girl is an established member of the group these "inappropriate" actions can come forth and are accepted, but when meeting for the first time, they make for a bad impression. Social inappropriateness is considered acceptable once a girl is an established friend.

Image

Image is what peers see to classify a girl as part of a social group. Image is composed of a girl's appearance, personality projection, the way that she carries herself (nonverbal communication), social skills and her self-confidence. It is not necessarily about beauty or physical attractiveness, but social appeal, and "look."

Option 1: Mainstream your Image

It is hard to say, but most typical girls will not be accepting of a girl whose image is too unusual or atypical. The majority of peers will not be accepting of girls who do not follow the basic rules and standards of hygiene and style. Girls who mainstream their image become part of the girl middle-class. Their options open to having more friends to choose from in the mainstream, and they also have the option of being friends with the unusual people instead of being confined to that class. Girls who reject mainstreaming and conformity generally have fewer choices because there are only a certain number of people who will be initially accepting and friendly to people who do not appear mainstream. In choosing acquaintances, people want friends who will fit in with their social group. If there are too many detracting things about a girl's image, peers will automatically cross her off the list, unless they can get to know her another way—which surpasses the Image Profiling.

Option 2: Stay within the Unique/Unusual
Rankings of the Social Hierarchy

If a girl with AS does not want to appear mainstream, that is okay, but she will have a more limited number of peers who will accept her or start friendships with her. It is important to figure out what a girl with AS can focus on as appealing and likeable traits in making friends, determining what her positive assets are, and what behaviors/traits detract as barriers to friendship. Not every girl has to be "girly" or involved in makeup and fashion, but even athletic girls and self-proclaimed "tomboys" follow the teen code of hygiene and wear hairstyles and clothes that are socially appropriate for their image.

When a typical girl looks at another girl, she decodes her image to determine what level of social status the girl belongs to. The peer then compares herself to that and decides if she should make an effort at friendliness. Most often, girls want to make friends with girls who are equal to or higher in social status than they are. If a girl with AS has an image that detracts rather than being appealing, it may be more difficult to make friends for this reason. The goal in Image is to be as moderate and mainstream in appeal as possible.

Image Profiling
Typical girls do Image Profiling, in which with one glance they determine whether a girl is:

1. Higher in social status than she is.
2. Equal in social status to her.
3. Lower in social status than she is. Peers look at physical accessories, a girl's markers, such as the brands she wears, her accessories, and hairstyle. I am not advocating wearing expensive labels, but simply to dress in a stylish way that is mainstream, not detracting. Peers perceive social status based on social skills, self-confidence, and image. Acceptance is contingent upon the peer group viewing the individual as valuable and as an equal. Peers are less accepting when they feel they are superior to the image of the girl with AS.

We all want to be considered equals or more. That is why understanding the importance of image is vital to success, because it is a way to protect against peer judgment. Creating a change in image is proactive against judgment. Peers will be less judgmental if there is less to judge.

Updating and Improving Image
Girls with AS do not necessarily need to buy the most high fashion clothes, but should wear clothes that are attractive and are viewed by peers as acceptable. This is a peer reality. Wearing detracting clothes is limiting. Most peers are very sensitive to being associated with people who dress in unfashionable or odd ways.

A girl whose image is foreign to her peers in appearance and appeal can become almost like a caricature. Peers do not want to be associated with "the girl with the grandma glasses" or "the wolf lover girl." Peers see each other like an artist creates a caricature, overemphasizing prominent features like a unibrow, big glasses, or odd clothing. Peers are sensitive to this because of the natural teen self-focus. Other teens judge a girl based on what friends she associates with. Only other people with unusual "caricatures" will be accepting of her, and this restricts opportunity.

Improving image and appeal can begin with a change in physical appearance, and continue with self-esteem, confidence building, and social skills intervention. Teen girls care greatly about appearance and something appearance or hygiene related could be the deal-breaker for a potential friendship with typical girls.

My friend Kelsey, a teen with AS, said that this is what helped begin her social acceptance:

> I used to look like more of a tomboy and didn't care about brushing my hair or fashion. When I learned how to do my makeup and went shopping, people responded positively to my new look. Boys especially! I got positive attention. Some people say, "If I change the way I look I am not being true to myself. You should like people for who they are on the inside." While this is true, it is not reality. People are friendlier when you look more mainstream. And you are still true to yourself even if you change something about the way you look. Girls with AS should ask themselves, "Is it who you really are or are you willing to change it for success?"

2. Understanding Where to Fit In—Social Structures

Once a girl with AS understands how the way she presents herself affects her acceptance, she needs to know where she should look to make friends. Typical teens abide by social rules and a social hierarchy even though it is an invisible structure.

The Popularity Hierarchy
Popular/Elite Groups

These teens are members of the most admired activities, sports that are highly attended, and coolest clubs. Depending on school and region, what is popular changes, but it is often the classic "cheerleaders/football players." Whoever belongs to this Popular group has what the other teens at school want. Girls in this group follow the latest in fashion/makeup trends and have an ease of social skills. Popular/Elite people may have acquaintances with teens in the Middle/Mainstream group.

Middle/Mainstream Groups
The average teen is a part of this group. This includes belonging to the other sports, clubs, activities that are less Popular/Elite but still respected and liked. Teens in this group are generally liked, or they just blend in with the crowd of Mainstream people. Middle/Mainstream teens may have Acquaintances in both the Popular/Elite group and the Unique/Unusual group.

Unique/Unusual Groups
Teens who are different from the Mainstream are a part of this group. They may be in clubs/sports/activities that the other groups view as unpopular, but these teens still find friendships, happiness, and an identity within this level. Teens in this group may be bullied/ostracized. Teens in this group may have acquaintances in the Middle/Mainstream group.

Kelsey told me about her social success in the Popularity Hierarchy:

> *It is possible to break through the social layers of popularity. Start small, lower down, and be friendly to everyone. I just started saying hey to people around campus who would say it back, and now after building on that, I have friends in many different groups.*

Understanding the structure of popularity at school is not intended to make a girl feel as though she does not measure up, but just makes sense of the reasons why attempts at friendship with people from higher groups are less successful than attempting friendships within her own range. It also explains why cliques treat each other differently. It is a way to make sense of and socially categorize a school with hundreds of students. Typical peers have an extreme sensitivity to the Popularity Hierarchy and when a girl with AS upsets the system by attempting to befriend beyond her limits of popularity, it is seen as inappropriate, as though she were upsetting a social law! If a girl with AS has dreams of Elite Popularity, she has to begin somewhere. She has to work her way up from whatever level she belongs to at the present and move up slowly; skipping up to the top is rare. It takes a lot of social skills and also a Popular/Elite person needs to accept her as "okay." Friendships at one level higher or lower are possible, but in order to potentially befriend a person from a Popular/Elite group, a girl has to at least be in a Middle/Mainstream group. Often people belonging to the Popular/Elite group will not befriend girls from any-where else. The reason to explain this to a girl with AS is to help her understand that a friendship attempt failure may not have been due to something she did or her fault, but just related to her trying to befriend someone whose expectations were out of her league.

The same goes for dating. My brother with AS kept asking the prettiest and most popular girls to date him—who wouldn't want to date someone beautiful and popular? However it was unsuccessful because he was at a different level in popularity than they were. When I explained the Levels of Popularity, that a cheerleader was not necessarily going to want to date him, even though he wanted to date her, he thought I was making the whole thing up. It may seem made up, but it is reality to typical teens. He was going to keep being unsuccessful if he did not abide by the hierarchy. The positive solution to the dilemma was that he could find nice, friendly girls who were "in his league" to at least begin developing dating skills with, and then see what happens.

Levels of Relationship

There are many theories on interpersonal relationships, but below is how I describe the typical relationship categories that teens experience. There is a hierarchy of *interaction* that typical peers are sensitive to, but that girls with AS may not be. This hierarchy is comprised of different Levels of Relationship. When a girl with AS is gossiped about by peers who say, "I just don't know her that well, she gives way too much information, she is very odd," etc., it is because the information shared, or the action done by the girl with AS, was inconsistent with their Level of Relationship as perceived by the peer.

Levels of Relationship
5. Close Friends
4. Friends
3. Acquaintances
2. Familiar Faces
1. Strangers

Close friends
Friends you have been close with for at least a few months are Close Friends. You know some of each other's life story and family situation. You may have been to each other's homes and possibly have spent time with each other's family. You trust each other and share emotions, problems, and feelings. You may also share common interests, or have a similar sense of humor. You spend time together at and outside of school and may refer to each other as "good friends" or "best friends."

Friends
These are people you spend time with in school and occasionally do things with outside of school. You may hang out with each other at lunchtime. You know about and share some details of each other's lives and interests, but nothing too secretive or personal. You generally see these people when socializing in larger groups of friends.

Acquaintances
You know these people from school, organizations, activities, classes, and may have conversations every so often, small talk, or school related. The only time you spend outside of school with these people is for mandatory group projects together, or for an event with a sport/club/activity you both take part in. You sometimes say "hi" to each other around campus, town, or at a school wide event. You both know each other's names.

Familiar Faces
These are people you have not spoken to, but you may know their name, or have seen them before. These people are different from Strangers because you can identify them by name or sight. They might be people from a class whom you have not spoken to directly, or friends of a friend. You may know who they are, but they may not know who you are, or your name.

Strangers
You have not seen, heard of, or met these people. You do not know each other. It is a nonexistent relationship.

Typical peers auto-categorize the people they know at school and in the community into these groups and that is why actions, jokes, comments, and conversations are "appropriate" to the listener based on how close (or distant) a relationship is with the speaker. Comments or stories are deemed by peers as inappropriate when the speaker says something that is not appropriate for the level of relationship they have to each other. Just because a girl is on a sports team, it does not mean that she is in equal standing in Levels of Relationship with all teammates. Some will remain her acquaintances, and others can grow into friendships.

Too Personal

Personal information needs to be given slowly and over time, allowing a trusting relationship to build until it grows from the level of Acquaintance to Friend. When a girl consistently makes too-personal comments, gives too much information, or tells a story in too much detail for the level of relationship, that is when peers sense that something is weird, and begin to think of the girl as odd, creepy, overwhelming, or obnoxious. It is difficult to distinguish levels in relationships but it is a skill that can be learned over time.

> *"She tells me way too personal information. I mean, I barely even know her."*
>
> *"I don't know why she talks to me. We had one class together four years ago!"*
>
> *"Does she know that we are not even friends? I wish she would stop hanging around."*
>
> *"I feel smothered by her, we just met. She calls me all the time, and I don't call back."*
>
> *"She tells me stories with way too much detail. I don't really care to listen that much."*

Everything can be said, but it just depends on who is listening. A girl's Level of Relationship with the listener is important for conversational success. The same information that is inappropriate with an Acquaintance would have been appropriate if shared with a Close Friend. A ten-minute-long account of a vacation is too detailed to tell to an Acquaintance who only wants to hear a 15-30 second "I had a great time in Europe." It is important for a girl with AS to establish guidelines and the appropriate time span for talking about a subject depending on their Level of Relationship.

A Close Friend might not mind hearing about Star Wars for 30 minutes, but it could cause the end of an Acquaintanceship. A girl with AS should practice retelling stories, or talking on a subject, based on whom the listener is. A trusted adult or peer mentor can discuss and establish what time limits are appropriate.

> *Close Friend:* "Europe was wonderful, I went to Paris, London, Madrid…"—*10 minutes*
>
> *Friend:* "Europe was wonderful, I went to Paris London, Madrid…"—*5 minutes*
>
> *Acquaintance:* "Europe was wonderful, I went to Paris, London, and Madrid."—*1 minute*

The above minutes are guidlines. If the listener continues to ask questions and makes comments that show interest, the speaker should continue. If the topic a girl wishes to talk about is a restrictive or repetitive interest often brought up, the amount of time comfortable for peers might be fewer minutes than a conversation with new information or a new story. A girl with AS can decide with a parent or professional what is appropriate for her age group and topic.

Sometimes girls with AS may believe that they are Friends or Close Friends with a Familiar Face or an Acquaintance. This can cause social upset and potential humiliation in front of peers. In order to be socially successful, a girl with AS needs to practice taking perspective, and although Theory of Mind makes this difficult, she will have to practice imagining what the other person thinks of her, possibly using visible data from her interactions with that person if the idea is not concrete enough. She might even list all of the people she knows and the interactions she has had with them, or a yes/no checklist.

When you say "hi" does she/he say "hi" back?   Yes   No

Do you see her/him only at school?   Yes   No

Do you eat and hang out together at lunchtime?   Yes   No

Does she/he call you on the phone at home?   Yes   No

Are you in a club or team with her/him, but only hang out then?   Yes   No

Does she/he invite you to hang out on weekends?   Yes   No

She needs to distinguish between interactions initiated by her, and interactions the peer initiated. Would a peer spontaneously say "hi" in passing down the hallway if she didn't always initiate it first?

Teaching Tool: The Sims

A tool that may be helpful in explaining this concept to a girl with AS is a computer game called *The Sims*. In the latest version of this reality-type computer game, this concept is represented visually. Levels of Relationship between the characters in colors ranging from dark green (Close Friend) to yellow (Acquaintance) to red (Stranger/Familiar Face). When characters make comments or actions that are inappropriate for the level of their relationship, you can see the character lose points with that friend with an exaggerated reaction. You can see other character's thoughts visually, in thought bubbles. Just as in reality, if enough friendship mistakes are made, a Friend could go back to being an Acquaintance. The game makes abstract concepts like these very visual and literal, using numbers and colors. It is a great tool for explanation, and could be generalized to real life situations.

Unfriendliness

It may also be necessary to make a list of people to avoid—bullies or unfriendly people who do unkind things. Sometimes it may be difficult for girls with AS to know when they are being made fun of, or their kindness is not reciprocated. For example, a girl may think that she has a friend because she calls her on the phone, but if that girl never returns her calls and displays avoidance behaviors, she needs to know when to stop before gossip or annoyed anger occurs.

I asked Kelsey what she thought other girls with AS could do if thinking about the Levels of Relationship was too abstract.

Kelsey suggested:

> When you see familiar faces, it does not mean that you are friends with that person. I used to go up to people I recognized from years ago in elementary school, or a familiar person from a class, and interact with them as if they were a best friend. It was unsuccessful. You have to think, "Was this person nice to you or were they not?" Make a list of nice things that friends do and things that are unfriendly. Only approach people who do nice things.

Making Friends

Making a new friend is making more than just a single friend. Girls travel in packs and have a group mentality. Most typical girls have more than one friend, so a girl with Asperger's needs to be wary of fitting in with the group structure her new friend already belongs to. The easiest friendship to make would be making friends with a girl who does not have any other friendship commitments, but that is a more rare situation.

Multiple Friends to Befriend

More often, a girl with AS's new friend will already belong to an existing social group, a clique that she will have to learn to navigate. Girls are insecure about losing friends and when a girl with AS suddenly joins the clique, peers wonder how this will change their role in the group structure.

Rosalind Wiseman, author of *Queen Bees and Wannabees,* has taught hundreds of teen girls and has come to see patterns in the roles that teen girls play in their group structures.

Wiseman classifies them as:

7 Common Roles Girls Play in Cliques

1. *The Queen Bee:* Through a combination of charisma, force, money, looks, will and manipulation, this girl reigns supreme over the other girls and weakens their friendships with others, thereby strengthening her own power and influence.

2. *The Sidekick:* She notices everything about the Queen Bee, because she wants to be her. She will do everything the Queen Bee says. The Queen Bee, as her best friend, makes her feel popular and included.

3. *The Floater:* She has friends in different groups and can move freely among them. She has influence over other girls but doesn't use it to make them feel bad.

4. *The Torn Bystander:* She's constantly conflicted about doing the right thing and her allegiance to the clique. As a result, she's the one most likely to be caught in the middle of a conflict between two girls or two groups of girls.

5. *The Pleaser/Wannabe/Messenger:* She will do anything to be in the good graces of the Queen Bee and the Sidekick. When two powerful girls, or two powerful groups of girls are in a fight, she is the go-between. However, the other girls eventually turn on her as well. She'll enthusiastically back them up no matter what. She can't tell the difference between what she wants and what the group wants.

6. *The Banker:* Girls trust her when she pumps them for information because it doesn't seem like gossip; instead, she does it in an innocent, "I'm trying to be your friend" way. This is the girl who sneaks under adult radar all the time because she can appear so cute and harmless.

7. *The Target:* She's the victim, set up by the other girls to be humiliated, made fun of, excluded. She can be part of a clique or outside the clique. Either way, she feels isolated and alone.

A new friend that a girl with AS makes could play any of these roles in the clique. It is important in blending into a group of girls to figure out the power structure and figure out if a girl with AS is breaking in on already existing and established friendships. She would not want to upset the Queen Bee, for example.

Social groups are organized and structured, and when a new person is brought into the group, the existing structure has to shift. So, if a girl with AS begins a new friendship and does not take into account and respect the roles and positions of the members of the group, she may not be accepted or may even be excluded. If a girl with AS is being brought into the clique by the Pleaser or Target, she has an uncertain new position because less stable members initiated the friendship. Sometimes, for a new person to successfully become integrated, a more influential member of the group, such as the Sidekick, needs to initiate. Thinking about structure is a less personal or hurtful way of thinking about girl friendships. When a girl with AS is not "clicking" with a group of girls, she should analyze what possible reasons, apart from her own actions, could have caused the lack of success. Sometimes it is about the other girls and their roles in the power structure.

The reason for explaining these three social structures is because they intertwine with each other. That is why it is difficult to fit in if a girl with AS does not automatically sense them as typical peers do. If a girl with AS does not understand one or more she is less adept for fitting in than a typical girl. Cliques exist at any level in the Popularity Hierarchy, have members in any of the Common Roles, and the girls within the clique may be at any Level of Relationship with each other. That is why it is difficult to navigate the teen social world as a girl with AS.

Tricky Situation: "Best Friends" Already

Girls change *best* friends less often than they shift most friendships. Girls confide most in their best friends and feel as though they have power because they have such a close connection—something most girls constantly search after. This security gives best friends confidence. It is emotional when best friendships end because there is so much trust and secrecy involved. It is a big deal in the girl world.

Sometimes a girl with AS may make new friends with a peer who already has a best friend. Being a new third party can create problems because the old best friend could be intimidated by the shift from a two-person structure to a three-person structure. The pair may have certain ways that they have always done things, and the girl with AS needs to be able to accept that she is a new member in the group, not best friend #3 yet. In this situation a girl with AS should be friendly to both, and keep in mind that the old best friend may feel intimidated by her, and may feel as though she is going to steal away her best friend. A good way to become friends with a girl and her best friend is to be casual about showing interest directly to one girl. Also, if there are other girls in the clique, the girl with AS should look for the girls who are not "claimed" or part of an exclusive best friend pair. Chances are that she feels insecure that she does not have a close or best friend, and she could be a good person to build a friendship with. A girl with AS needs to come to an already-best-friendship with the expectation that the other two will choose each other and she will not always be included.

Disclosing Asperger's Syndrome to Friends

Disclosing Asperger's Syndrome is something that requires planned and careful consideration. Girls should consult trusted adults for guidance, and discuss what to say. Disclosing can lead to many different outcomes, and often depend on who the peers are as individuals, and how the information on Asperger's is presented. For example, a professional explained to my brother's choir that he has AS after they had a few weeks to get to know him without knowledge of his Asperger's. They had indeed noticed differences about him, and the professional was able to make sense of what the students had observed in the context of his diagnosis. It was successful, and the students were understanding. There are many different ways to disclose. It is possible that classmates have already noticed a social difference, and disclosure provides a logical and legitimate explanation for what they have noticed, and prevents them from continuing to form inaccurate opinions.

Also important to consider is the amount of time and Level of Relationship a girl has with the peers she wishes to disclose to. Feeling out when and how to disclose is a social skill in itself. Some outcomes may be positive, such as the experience my brother had, yet the outcome may be far different if a girl discloses to untrustworthy people. She may believe she is among friends when, in fact, she is not. Some girls who disclose their Asperger's Syndrome become even more targeted. Students could use that information as fuel for teasing and gossiping. A girl with Asperger's should be very sure she can trust a person before disclosing to him/her. It may be something close friends should know and understand, but it isn't always necessary for everyone in the classroom to know. Sharing personal information with the wrong person could result in a social stigma that could last for years. It needs to be accurate information explained in the right way, and to true friends who have genuine interest in the acceptance and understanding of their friend with Asperger's Syndrome.

Sometimes it is hard to tell if letting your friends know that you have AS would help socially. Will it make it easier to fit in?

Kelsey said:

One of the things that helped me the most was telling my friends after a month or two of knowing them that I had a learning disability and sometimes I may do things in social situations that are unexpected. I tell them that it is okay to correct me, and tell me when I do something wrong, because I want to improve. When friends are upset at me and I don't know why, I ask another person, "Did I do something wrong? What social error did I make?" I have to work on being receptive and listening to their feedback.

3. Meeting Social Expectations

Typical girls have specific social expectations of each other. They expect that other girls know what to do and how to be a good friend. When a teen girl asks, "Do I look fat?" The answer is always no! White lying is an important friendship skill to have in maintaining the fragile self esteem of teen girls. If a girl with AS does not know what the expectations are, her friends may think that she doesn't care about maintaining their friendship.

How Typical Girls Show Interest in Each Other

When an Acquaintanceship is established, the way to move it toward Friendship is by showing interest. A Friendship could move to a Close Friendship by showing consistent interest.

Typical girls show interest by:
- Calling each other on the phone
- Spending time at lunch together
- Spending time after school together, going places
- Hanging out at each other's houses
- Joining extracurricular activities together
- Writing notes
- Giving compliments
- Sharing and keeping secrets
- Gossiping about others
  (yes, girls use others' drama and secrets to bond)
- Sending each other text messages
- Instant messaging
- Leaving online comments on Blogs, Livejournals, Facebook, Xanga, and Myspace webpages
- Leaving complimentary picture comments on Myspace photos
- Having inside jokes.

Technology such as the internet and cell phones has shifted the ways that friendships form. Most teens spend time after school online instant messaging multiple friends at once. That means that they can show interest to more friends more instantaneously than the traditional methods of a phone or paper note. Seeing these signs of interest is threatening to girls who are not in on the action. Seeing friends leaving each other comments on MySpace can cause a girl to feel left out.

If a girl with AS has control, she should invite all of the established friends of a clique when doing things outside of school; that way everyone feels included, and part of the growth of the new friendship. During these group outings is the ideal time to give a positive impression to all the girls in the established group in order to blend in.

A girl with AS should know how to show interest in these ways and work with a peer, parent, or professional on knowing the right things to say in each medium of technology.

Kelsey said:

> Most girls don't want to talk about science or Star Wars. Find something to contribute to what girls talk about. Listen until you can contribute instead of just interrupting with the topic you want to talk about. It is better to be thought of as shy and quiet than loud and obnoxious. I stayed back from conversations and just observed for a very long time until I felt ready.

What Girls Talk About: Be in the Know

Boys, fashion, shopping, movies, and music will always be teen topics of conversation, and often girls will get their information on what is most current through television, the internet, and magazines.

The Teen Channels

Most teens watch hours of MTV. If you want to do some research on popular music and teen culture, watch MTV's Total Request Live (TRL), and see the ten most popular music groups of the moment as deemed by America's teens. You can look to the artists or teens in the audience for fashion inspiration. You can also see throughout the day the other MTV programs that teens are watching. Bringing up, "Can you believe that ____ is #1 on TRL?" or, "Did you see ____'s brand new video?" in conversation is a good way to show that a girl is current. Watch the TV network E! to find out about what is going on with celebrities and fashion, another popular girl topic. A contribution to conversation would be "Did you hear _____ broke up?" "Did you see the dress _____ wore to the Oscars?" "Did you hear what _____ named her baby?!"

The television network, the CW, specifically targets programming towards teens. The latest and most popular primetime television shows (8:00-10:00 p.m.) on various television networks also come up in conversation. Sometimes teen girls will watch a favorite show together as a weekly social event.

Depending on what kinds of social group a girl belongs to, topics of conversation vary. Some girls are not interested in pop culture. If a girl is part of a social group that does not watch TV, or prefers to talk about politics, news, sports, literature, or the environment, she should contribute on those topics. The overall message is that most teens are generalists and know a little about many different topics.

Many girls with AS are specialists, with greater knowledge about one or two topics. Many high schools have clubs and organizations devoted to specific interest groups such as Japanimae and science fiction. Most high schools allow for students to start their own clubs, and that is a good way to find other like-minded specialists on a subject.

Girls with AS will need the conversational and life skill of being well-informed about many areas of pop culture and current events. She will need to be good at "small talk" conversation so that others may perceive her as a pleasant person in the university dormitories, classroom, and at her workplace. Having conversational skills and being a specialist is a great asset. When she goes to college, she can choose a major and meet others with a similar favorite topic of conversation, and be a specialist in her field.

www.Wikipedia.org
Wikipedia is an online encyclopedia where you can learn about any subject in pop culture, and can also be used as a typical encyclopedia. If a girl does not know about a person, TV show, topic, singer, etc., that frequently comes

up in conversation, she can look it up in Wikipedia and have the entire history and related links.

Building Friendships

The way to begin to build friendships is to start with Familiar Faces/Acquaintances and go from there.

Teens, when walking around school, get into a rhythm of greeting Acquaintances to show that they acknowledge their presence by making eye contact and saying "Hey, how are you?" "Good, how are you?" as they walk by each other.

No one tells the reality of their feelings ("My dog died, and I am so depressed!") Saying you are fine is just a courtesy and acknowledgement.

> *Scenario: Walking around campus you see a Familiar Face/ Acquaintance from a class or activity. Greet them.*
>
> *Action: Say, "Hey" or "Hi" in a casual way.*
>
> "Hi." ⟶ "Hi."
>
> *If they respond, do it again the next time you see them.*
>
> *Next try the scripted question, "Hey, how are you?"*
>
> "Hey, how are you?" ⟶ "Good, how are you?"
>
> *If they say "Good, how are you?" you say "Good, thanks" and keep walking.*

When a girl has developed an acquaintanceship she can turn it into a friendship by bringing in daily conversation. If a girl sees a classmate at a basketball game and says "Hey Katie, how are you?" it establishes that Katie has seen her there and she can talk to her about the game the next day in class. The next day in class she can ask her open, non-yes/no questions like "What did you think of____" (What did you think of the game?) What did you think of the shootout?) From there the topic can be shifted to other topics such as sports, players on the team, other classmates at the game, etc.

From a scripted and cordial greeting to a classmate, a girl can establish herself as present at an event. From presence at that shared event she can talk with the classmate about a shared experience (excitement, delight, shock, etc.) and then move to common interest topics that can build friendship and rapport.

Responsiveness

Sometimes people with AS have a harder time distinguishing responsiveness. A typical peer's claims of being "stalked and smothered" are a sign that a person with AS has a difficult time telling when interactions with a peer are responsive or avoidance behaviors. Friendship is like a game of tennis; if you are the one serving the ball all the time and no one is hitting it back—it is not a real game. Girls need to learn to wait for a friend to call or message back to avoid making her feeling nagged. If the girl's "friend" never calls back and she doesn't want to wait anymore, she needs to figure out if there is a reason the other girl does not respond. Friends should treat a girl nicely and make an effort. Teen girls are not likely to be confrontational about disliking a girl; more often they slowly and silently ignore and exclude. It is important for a girl with AS to brainstorm with a parent or professional a list of ways that teens show disinterest. If she sees these signs she should determine if she should confront her "friends," or take the hint and look elsewhere for friendship.

Some ways teens show disinterest:
- Avoiding
- Not returning phone calls
- Pretending not to see you walking by
- Ignoring
- Not responding to emails, text messages, or instant messages
- Not inviting you when the clique hangs out.

Circular Conversations

Teens hang out in circles to chat, which makes greeting and entering a conversation more complex than a one-on-one formal adult "say hello and shake hands," because everyone is facing inward. It is possible to tactfully enter a circular conversation.

Step 1.
The first step to being allowed into the circle is to silently and quickly survey who is in the circle and think about their Level of Relationship to you. Friend? Acquaintance?

Step 2.
When approaching the group casually walk up to the person with whom you have the highest Level of Relationship. Stand near them so you are in their peripheral vision. Greet them, and make eye contact.

Step 3.
If they are interested in making small talk they should open their body language to you and greet you. When you also open your body language toward your conversational partner you become a greater part of the circle. Greet others in the circle and then listen to the conversation that is already going on. Join in when you can contribute to a topic.

A Close Friend is more likely to open the circle to a girl than an Acquaintance or a Familiar Face. If a girl with AS stands next to or tries to break into the conversation through an Acquaintance or Familiar Face, she will have less success. If a girl with AS sees a friend but does not stand near to her she will not open her body to let the girl in. Positioning is key. Some Teen Greetings: "Hey" "Hi" "Hey, what's up?" "Hey, how's it goin'" "Hey guys! What's goin' on?" "Hi, how are you?" Find out what teens in your town say. Ethnicity and gender are also determining factors as to what greeting are appropriate.

Lunch Table Trauma
This idea is also suitable for lunch tables. Pick the person sitting at the table that you know best and greet them. If there isn't room to sit next to her, sit at the end of the table where you can talk to her and be integrated into the conversation. If they say there isn't room, don't appear upset; say, "Oh, okay, maybe next time." Move around the lunch area casually greeting your next Close Friend, then ask Friends, then ask Acquaintances. If no one will let you eat with them, go to a friendly teacher's classroom, the library, a club/organization that meets that day at lunch, or find a place out of view and read a book and eat. Work on a strategy to be proactive, make a plan, and figure out whom to eat with

next time. If you have a Friend in the class period before lunch, walk with her to lunch and eat together. If she is reluctant, perhaps you are only Acquaintances, or she worries about the structure and lunch plan of her existing social group. Sometimes girls plan to meet each other at a certain location before walking to the cafeteria together. Some groups of friends have an understood location where they eat lunch every day together as a group.

What if They Aren't Interested?

If they are not interested in saying anything beyond, "Hi, how are you?" or ignore you, if they do not open up their body language to include you, it is time to make an exit. Do not stand for more than ten seconds with no one responding to your existence. Say one of the following to the person you greeted:

"Okay, well, I'll see you later."

"Be right back."

"Excuse me for a sec."

"I have to go to____."

"Well, nice to see you, I'll talk to ya later."

"I think I'm gonna go ____(get a drink, get something to eat, go to my locker, etc). See ya later."

Do not come back to talk to them later. It is an exit, to save face, and to let them know that you have better things to do than be ignored by them.

Kelsey suggests:
When you go up to a group of people and say "hi" if the person you greet only looks over their shoulder to say "hi" and doesn't open up the circle, they don't want to include you. Instead of standing there, say, "Talk to you later," "See ya later," or "Bye" and leave if the conversation fizzles. Go get a drink, snack, visit other acquaintances until you get a responsive group.

Sticking Together

Younger teen girls generally equate being seen by peers without friends as being momentarily friendless. This accounts for their desire for their friends to accompany them everywhere. Being alone = being a-loner.

Also, accompanying a friend is a way to show interest with little effort. Girls show interest in accompanying each other places, such as the classic, "Will you come with me to the bathroom?" and also, "Will you walk with me…[to my locker, the cafeteria line, to talk to guys, to class, to ask a teacher a question, etc.]. None of this accompanying seems to be too interesting to the girl who is the accompanier, but it is a show of security and support to the friend she accompanies. It is also a gesture of interest and friendship. However, girls with AS need to know for safety reasons in what situations accompanying a friend somewhere could be a manipulation of her friendship and a dangerous, illegal, or criminal situation.

Girls with AS who spend lunchtime by themselves should practice looking content and busy in being alone. No typical peers want to befriend a person who is a sulky "loner." The only legitimate reason teens accept for being alone at lunch is because of school obligations—forgot to do reading or an assignment and need to catch up quickly before class. Reading a book confidently or starting homework early is better than sitting alone or staring at people. Another way to stay included is to find out when clubs and organizations meet and join the ones that are interesting, or start a new one.

Some skills that girls with AS need to master in order to be friends with typical girls are related to emotion, confidentiality, loyalty, and self esteem. Girls like to be with girls who make them feel good about themselves, and enhance their self-esteem.

Girls with AS should practice conversational skills so they know: where to stand, signs of disinterest, how to contribute positively to conversation, how long and often to make eye contact, appropriate loudness, personal space, and how to exit a boring conversation politely. Girls should also know the facial expression and eye contact cues that peers give when they are bored with a topic of conversation.

Facial Expressions

Know what facial expressions and body language mean, "I am friendly and approachable," and those that look like, "I am angry, don't interact with me."

In conversation she should nod her head to show she is listening and casually make eye contact every 10 seconds and look away for 5-10 seconds. She shouldn't stare, but she should also not avoid eye contact. She should glance at the speaker occasionally to let her know that she is still attentive to the coversation topic.

In consoling a friend she should be able to appear concerned and show support.

Kelsey used to hunch back in her chair and dart piercing stares at others around the room: *I didn't know that I was frowning a lot and had an angry look on my face in class. When you look mad, no one wants to talk to you or be friendly.*

4. Bullying and Mean Girls

Facing bullies is really intimidating and unfortunately some girl bullies are relentless. Gossiping, rumor spreading and cattiness are so prevalent that popular movies such as *Mean Girls* have been made as a response. *Mean Girls* popularized the term and also the title "Queen Bee." Now the term "Mean Girls" is freely used to express girl bullying in a new way. The movie *Mean Girls* is based on the book *Queen Bees and Wannabees*. The book is a great resource for parents and adolescent girls. It has in-depth strategies for handling girl bullying, fitting in, and related issues. Another great resource for helping adolescent girls through tough friendship and school situations are the award-winning American Girl books, *The "Smart Girl" Guide to Friendship Troubles, Guide to Sticky Situations* and *Guide to Middle School*. They are wonderful books that were compiled from the questions received from hundreds of girls. They tackle every friendship issue imaginable with advice from peers and experts.

From *Queen Bees and Wannabees*:

> **Teasing:** *Bad teasing happens both inside and out of the clique, and either way, it's ugly. The teasing is done precisely to put the recipient in her place. First, she's relentlessly teased about something she's insecure about; girls always seem to know exactly what to say to cause the most humiliation. Second, she's dismissed or put down when she defends herself ("Can't you take a joke?" "What are you making such a big deal of this for?"). Often the result is that she ends up apologizing for speaking up in the first place ("I'm sorry, I'm such an idiot") or swallowing it lest she lose her place in the clique.*

Gossiping: *Along with teasing, gossiping is one of the fundamental weapons that girls use to humiliate each other and reinforce their own social status. Gossip is so humiliating because girls' natural self-focus means that they literally feel like the whole world notices everything they do, and what's said about them and their social status in school often serves as the basis for their self-identity. What do girls gossip about? In middle school: conflicts with friends, rivalries between cliques, boys and crushes; in high school: who had sex at the last party, who got drunk or did drugs, who's getting used.*

From *Queen Bees and Wannabes* by Rosalind Wiseman, copyright © 2002 by Rosalind Wiseman. Used by permission of Crown Publishers, a division of Random House, Inc.

Author Rosalind Wiseman suggests to parents ways that a girl can solve a situation involving gossip or rumor spreading:

- Your daughter can confront the Mean Girl.
- She can ask a teacher or counselor for help.
- You can call the Mean Girl's parents.
- You can talk to the teacher.
- You can talk to an administrator.

The book provides in-depth ways to approach each confrontation.

Sometimes it is easier for girls to think that a Mean Girl brings out someone else's insecurities to mask her own troubles. In the dozens of people I asked, most people thought these were reasons girls bully:

- Jealousy
- Self-esteem
- Power building
- Status and respect through fear
- Insecurity.

Comebacks

The only way a comeback to a Mean Girl can be effective is if it is said with fearless but non-confrontational confidence. It needs to be said matter-of-factly, with ease in a "so what?" kind of way. Not questioning her power, but just affirming that you obviously know about the insecurity she is pointing out. Girls with Asperger's Syndrome need to practice conversation-stopping comebacks with adults to build their confidence against bullies.

Mean Girl Insult: "You have the ugliest glasses and you're so fat."

Megan, a girl with AS, suggests a conversation stopper like:
   "Thanks for letting me know."

Megan also suggested ignoring:
   I was bullied for having an under-bite and some guys made fun of me. I just ignored them and continued on with what I was already doing. They couldn't tell if I was really ignoring them or if I didn't hear their remarks and eventually stopped.

Typical Girls Overcome Bullying Too

I asked my typical friends and acquaintances who had been victims of bullying how they stopped it and what advice they would have for girls who were being bullied.

In Trying to Make Friends

"Joining Band in junior high really helped me connect with lots of different people, I always had friends and people that I had similar interests with and that really helped me to fit in during high school."

– Carly

"In my experience, if one really needs a friend it actually makes it harder to make one, simply because such a person is looking to take something from a relationship, not give something to it."

– Candice

"You may not get along with everyone, but there are other people like you somewhere that you will get along with. I was lucky enough to find them in choir and theatre. It's people that are like me."

– Rachel

Why do people bully?

"I believe that all bullies grow out of anger plus insecurity, and the really bad ones have no idea that what they are doing is wrong because this is the way they are treated at home. Since at home they are the loser, they must become the winner in the world outside their home."

– Kris

"Because it's easy to pick on people who don't defend themselves, in a way picking on people protects the person from getting picked on themselves."

– Carly

"They have control or security issues stemming from their families. Maybe they are bullied by their older brothers or sisters and feel the need to gain some kind of control by bullying others outside of their home element."

– Jill

How did you stop the bullying?

What I did to stop it was to develop individual friends in different groups, and that created a shift in the "group think" because if one person in a group thinks you are okay, and will talk to you in the hall or outside of school, the group sees that you are okay and will treat you that way.

– Kris

"Building confidence and skills in a sport, club, or activity helps. They could pick on me all they wanted but when I stepped on a softball field I was the best and they could never take that away from me."

– Jill

"What really helped me minimize bullying was by showing them it didn't affect me. It was always a guilty pleasure to watch a bully become unsatisfied and frustrated when their taunting isn't ignored but rather turned against them.... I was taught to kill them with kindness. Just be as sweet as you possibly can be. Make them believe that you are completely oblivious to their jabs."

– Brittany

"I was definitely picked on for being fat. Although I was bullied a lot, I never let it get to me because I was a stronger person than that. I think

that people who get made fun of tend to keep the mean comments with them and start to believe them because of the repetitive nature of bullying. I also knew in my mind that letting what they say stick in my mind will not make things any better; if I was going to be happy with who I was I needed to let it go and have my family and friends at my side. The true way I overcame being bullied was I changed myself, and got healthier, not for everyone else, but to make myself happier."

— Lauren

"I tried to stay positive as much as possible. I stayed away from those mean girls as much as I could, I became closer friends with some other girls, and tried to spare my own feelings by not thinking about how much hurt I was feeling. I didn't ignore the other girls (because that would mean they had won!) but decided to be as nice to them as possible and try not to show how sad I actually was."

— Krissy

Online Bullying
Cyber bullies
Bullies who use the internet and technology to be mean and hurtful to their targets, often anonymously.

Instant Messaging
Using a program like AOL, Yahoo, Google, or MSN Instant Messenger, teens send instant emails to each other. Usually one-sentence-long messages, they can "chat" with several friends at once. If you are being bullied on instant messenger you can use the "block" feature to stop Cyber bullies. Get a different screen name and only tell friends about it.

Blogs/Livejournals/Xanga
Online diaries in which teens post journal entries about their thoughts. Others can see them and comment. Cyber bullies leave anonymous mean comments. Make your journal "Friends only" or "Private" so only people you pick can see your posts. Also, only people who post with a screen name can comment on your page.

Myspace/Facebook
The most popular and fastest growing sites because they are more fun, interactive, and visual than email. Teens can post pictures of themselves,

email each other and leave comments on each other's pages and pictures. Teens choose who their "Top 8" closest friends to display on their personal page will be. On Facebook, teens are grouped by high school, university, or city. Facebook has good privacy settings, so use all of them. To protect against Cyberbullies make your profile "Private" and "Approve Comments Before Posting"

Safety is important and sometimes girls with AS might not see the ulterior motives of an online friend. It is important to teach girls with AS online safety: never posting an address, last name, or telephone number online; only giving information over the internet to trusted real-life friends, not people met online; and never meeting an online friend in person, at least not without her parent being present. I know girls with AS who have been vicitmized. In sharing this information, I hope to prevent it from happening again.

In general girls with AS should be careful who they choose friendships with.

Megan added:

> It is important that you are careful who you choose to be friends with, they could be using you or get you into trouble, or even involved with drugs and alcohol. Don't fold into peer pressure or get in dangerous situations.

Girls with AS are bright and beautiful and have intellect, talents, and skills that many typical peers wish they had. The important thing for girls to remember is that bullying will stop, even if it seems never ending in the present. Girls with AS should get the right supports, go to college, and be respected and successful in a field, to study the interest that was once a barrier in high school.

Resources

The Sims and *The Sims 2* PC game

Urbandictionary.com

Wikipedia.org

Mean Girls on DVD

Books

Crisswell, Patti Kelley, and Angela Martini. *A Smart Girl's Guide to Friendship Troubles.* Wisconsin: American Girl Library, 2003.

Wiseman, Roselind. *Queen Bees & Wannabes: Helping Your Daughter Survive Cliques, Gossip, Boyfriends & Other Realities of Adolescence.* New York: Three Rivers Press, 2002.

I would like to thank the following people for their input and inspiration: Kelsey Leathers, Meghan McQuitty, Jill Schock, Brianna Duffy, Kris Feldman, Krissy France, Tom Lund, Bradley Markano, Lauren Mowry, Brittany Oliphant, and Carly Schmidt. Thank you to my family and especially to my brother, Tom.

For more information, visit *www.lisailand.com.*

Preparing for Puberty and Beyond

Meet Mary Wrobel, MA CSS/SLP

A teacher and Speech-Language Pathologist, Mary Wrobel has been working with students with autism or Asperger's Syndrome for more than fifteen years. She wrote *Taking Care of Myself: A Personal Curriculum for Young People with Autism/Asperger's* to help teach students with disabilities how to live safe, healthy lives. She also trains both parents and professionals in the area of puberty and its accompanying safety, cleanliness, and health issues.

She is a well-known speaker on the lecture circuit, as well as a consultant to many schools. She is well versed in a number of treatment modalities, such as ABA and Floortime, among others.

Having "that talk" with typical girls is difficult enough for parents; it can be even more stressful for parents of Asperger's girls—and for the girls themselves. But it's a mistake to believe that they will have already "picked up" information about menstruation and sex from their peers (or even from sex-education classes), as many "typical" girls do. Therefore, Mary Wrobel emphasizes, it is important to begin preparing Asperger's girls early on about what physical, mental, and emotional changes to expect as they enter puberty, and how to handle them.

When dealing with parents whose daughters are about to enter puberty, I typically experience two types of mothers. Either a given mother may be in denial that her daughter with Asperger's is getting older and is about to begin menstruation, or the mother is in a panic as to how to teach and prepare her daughter for puberty. The rule of thumb is that all girls will go through puberty, and given the current trend of physical maturation, often sooner than we think. As parents and educators, we need to know what to expect, and plan how to instruct our pre-adolescent girls on the puberty changes that will occur. We need to be prepared for teaching these important changes to girls with Asperger's.

Understanding Changes During Puberty

Puberty is not an easy transition for anyone, let alone an individual with Asperger's. Most of us think of puberty as the physical changes that occur when a girl becomes a woman. But puberty involves more than just physical development and menstruation. Puberty consists of physical, emotional and mental changes during an individual's adolescent years, as that person transitions from childhood to adulthood. Puberty doesn't occur overnight, but takes many years to complete, often beginning as young as nine years old for some girls, and typically ending before the age of eighteen.

Most of us know what physical changes to expect during puberty, such as height increase and weight gain, followed by pubic, leg and underarm hair growth, breast development, enhanced hip-to-waist ratio, and menstruation. What is less known are the mental and emotional changes that occur during puberty, which are typical of all adolescents, not just individuals with Asperger's.

Many of the changes during puberty are due to the increase of hormones in an adolescent's body. This increase in hormones will cause emotional changes, such as mood swings, increased anxiety, depression, insecurity, and impulsivity. Emotional outbursts are common during puberty, as are acts of defiance and aggression. Sometimes self-injurious behavior may occur.

Mental changes are likely to occur as well. Changes in priorities and interests are common, as well as possible obsessive-compulsive tendencies. Adolescents may experience difficulty concentrating, and focusing their attention. Some adolescents may become more communicative, whereas others will withdraw, and communicate less. On top of all this there will probably be an increased interest in the opposite sex and sexuality in general.

All these changes in how teenage girls with Asperger's are feeling, thinking and reacting can be frustrating and confusing to them, as well as to adults. They don't know why they feel different, uncomfortable and possibly upset. They may be frightened about the changes that are taking place in their bodies and minds. It becomes necessary for parents and educators to explain the emotional and mental changes that are occurring, and reassure these adolescent girls that what they are experiencing is normal, and that they can talk about the things that are bothering them. However, as responsible adults, if you notice a significant increase in anxiety or depression, you should consider consulting a doctor.

If your student or child has significant behavioral and emotional difficulties before puberty, then it is likely those behaviors will become worse as they enter their adolescent years. It's important, therefore, to address behavior concerns before students enter puberty. We need to teach students to understand and communicate their feelings appropriately. Students need to learn strategies to practice patience and flexibility. And they need to be able to self-calm. It goes without saying that physical aggression towards others should not be tolerated. As kids get bigger and stronger, they must find appropriate ways to express their anger and frustration, other than physical aggression towards others and destruction of property.

Traditional Puberty Instruction

Teaching about sex, puberty and menstruation has long been the job of the public school system. Most parents depend on the curriculum and instruction from their child's school to cover those puberty topics that many parents are uncomfortable teaching. These days, other than buying the necessary products for their daughter's menstruation and hygiene, most parents of neurotypical girls don't need to worry about how to instruct their children on the basics.

Contrary to what we may think, typical puberty instruction in public schools consists of a brief presentation, usually in the form of a movie, with a question and answer session following. Puberty instruction may occur in a two hour session, or be spread out over a few days, usually sometime during the course of fifth or sixth grade. The puberty instruction is typically facilitated by a school nurse, or a few hardy teachers who are willing to take on the challenge. Most of these movies are more an introduction to basic puberty changes than actual in-depth sex education instruction, which may come later in high school health or biology classes. Most often the movies and discussions simply pique the interest of the students and get them thinking and talking. The real education comes from the research and the discussion among the students themselves.

Most kids are anxious to learn all they can about puberty and sex, and will search for answers, and discuss these topics in-depth with their peers. Most neurotypical students have been thinking about and discussing these important topics with their friends, often long before their formal instruction. Young girls and boys have been watching older siblings and parents, reading books, watching movies and getting glimpses of puberty and sex from a variety of sources, sometimes several years before they experience puberty themselves. When formal puberty instruction finally arrives, they are usually ready with lots of ideas and questions.

Students with Asperger's, on the other hand, typically don't think about these issues before or during the time they are undergoing puberty, and are often clueless of the discussions of their peers. Like their neurotypical peers they too will probably receive the basic puberty and sex education instruction in school, but the information may be too much for them to understand or they will have little interest in it. Therefore, it becomes necessary to provide additional and more specific instruction to girls with Asperger's, either one-on-one or in small groups, to help them prepare for puberty.

Demonstrating Modesty and Hygiene Skills

Since girls with Asperger's obviously need to understand and demonstrate appropriate puberty skills, especially with regards to their menstruation and hygiene, we should start our basic instruction with self-help skills. Girls should definitely be bathing and dressing themselves long before they reach puberty. This means they should be able to do those self-help skills without help from others in the privacy of their bathroom and bedroom. Likewise, they should understand and demonstrate modesty and privacy by the age of eight or nine. They need to know that areas of their body covered by a swimsuit or underwear are considered private areas and are not to be seen by others. When teaching the concept of modesty, keep the rules simple. For example, when they are naked or dressing, they should be alone in their bedroom or bathroom, or in some cases a bathroom stall, with the door closed. By teaching these skills early on, you are laying the groundwork for discretion and personal safety before they begin puberty.

Good hygiene skills are also important before puberty begins. Girls need to be showering every day, with warm water, soap and shampoo. This is important because as they get older and enter puberty, their bodies will secrete more oils and perspiration, causing odor. If young girls already have the habit of bathing every day, then you won't have to address that issue along with new hygiene routines, such as using deodorant and wearing a bra, when they begin puberty.

If you know that your student or child has a hard time with change of any kind, then begin as early as possible with these changes. In other words, do not wait to introduce deodorant and bra use until she actually needs it. Getting used to wearing deodorant and a bra every day will likely take time. Always have your daughter choose the deodorant and style of bra to wear herself, as many individuals with Asperger's are sensitive to smells and tactile sensations. She may try lots of different deodorants and bras before finding the right one, but ultimately she will know better than anyone else what she likes or can tolerate.

Tracking Physical Development

After tackling the issues of hygiene, modesty and privacy, and long before she actually shows signs of physical development, you will want to begin instructing your daughter or student on the actual changes of puberty. I have been told by a number of nurses that there are subtle signs of physical change we need to watch for. Approximately nine to eleven months after a young girl develops breast buds, or what appears to be a true nipple, even in the absence of a developed breast, she will begin menstruation. Also during that time, or just before, she will begin to grow pubic hair. Underarm hair may not develop until she actually begins menstruation. If your daughter is demonstrating modesty, as she should, but you notice that the hair on her legs has become noticeably darker and thicker, then that would also indicate that she has pubic hair growth. It's wise for parents to always check with the pediatrician to know the exact development timeline for your daughter. Likewise, teachers should always check with parents and work closely with them during puberty instruction.

Teaching Physical Growth and Development

Begin instructing about the basic changes to their bodies as they mature. Use visuals, such as a line-drawn body progression chart that shows how the body slowly changes from child to adult woman. Many girls with Asperger's may have no idea how their naked body will look and change during the course of puberty. And since they don't typically have a visual reference for this, it's important to provide them with the step-by-step visuals to help them understand how the changes will occur and what the end result will look like. Talk about hair and breast growth, as well as how their figure will change with more defined hips. Explain that all girls go through this change and that it's okay and necessary as they get older. Emphasize cleanliness and privacy, and instill the habit of routine deodorant use on clean underarms, as well as wearing a clean bra every day.

Anticipate the questions and concerns they may have, and give simple, basic information. Don't be tempted to give tangential information when first instructing about their physical development. Too much information or associated topics may cause confusion at this point. Later on, as girls comprehend and progress through the stages of puberty, you may want to discuss male stages of development, or other related topics. During the course of your instruction, don't always assume that they understand what you are telling them. Have them retell information they have learned and answer specific questions.

I would recommend using visuals, such as abstract pictures or photos as much as possible. Individuals on the autism spectrum tend to be visual learners, and need a visual reference in order to fully comprehend new information. Even highly intelligent, verbal individuals with Asperger's will need, or at least benefit from, visual supports during instruction.

Preparing for Menstruation

Approximately six months to a year before you know they should begin having a period, introduce menstruation and give the basics of what it is and what they need to do. In other words, talk about blood coming from their vagina and flowing between their legs. Explain that this blood only means they are having their period. They are not hurt when the blood comes, but it will be messy and they need to wear pads to keep the messy blood from getting on their panties and clothing, etc. Keep the facts simple at first. For example, blood will come each month, or about every twenty-eight days, and will flow for five or six days, and then stop. We need to wear pads in our panties while blood is coming out of our vaginas. We change our pads in the bathroom when they become dirty with blood, and we should avoid touching the blood on the pad. We fold and throw the dirty pads away in the appropriate trash cans and we wash our hands after we change our pads. It's also important to remind girls to bathe well during their period, because menstruation contributes to the dirt and odor of their bodies.

When instructing about the basics of menstruation, it's helpful to create a social-story type book, using the student's name, along with illustrations, such as abstract pictures or realistic photos, to explain their period. A story is a good way to remind them of what will happen when they get their period. And by including an individual's name throughout the story or book, a girl will feel it is truly about her.

When teaching about menstruation, use actual pads and allow girls to practice putting the pads in and taking them out of a given pair of panties that have not been worn by anyone. The practice will familiarize them with the feel of the pads, and how to take off the protective strip and position the pad inside the panties, as well as learning to sequence the steps to pad changing. To produce authentic looking blood during practice sessions, use red food coloring on the pad. The red food coloring looks surprisingly realistic and will prepare them for actual blood on their pads. This is important because not only do they need a realistic visual of what it will look like, but many girls are afraid of blood, and this will help to desensitize them to the real thing.

Since many girls with Asperger's have sensory issues as well as difficulty with change, have your child or student practice wearing a pad for longer periods of time to get used to the feel of it in their panties before they actually have their period. Always allow your child to choose the type of pad she wants. If she is given the choice of selecting the type of pads herself, she is more likely to wear them.

Again, it is not necessary at this time to teach young girls about the biology of menstruation, reproduction, childbirth, or sexual intercourse. Those topics can be discussed at a later time, when a student is older and more mature, and ready to digest that information. Learning the basics about menstruation and learning to take care of themselves during their periods may be more than enough for girls to handle at this stage in their lives. Nonetheless, all of this instruction may take time, so be prepared to repeat lessons. Encourage them to ask questions, quiz them on what will happen and what they need to do.

Prepare girls for the discomforts of menstruation. We don't often think about cramping, bloating, menstrual headaches and PMS until we actually have those discomforts. But girls with Asperger's may not associate those problems with getting their periods, and we can't assume they will make that connection, or be able to problem-solve on their own, when they have various menstrual difficulties. Discuss with your daughter or student the various problems that could arise and give her specific solutions for dealing with them.

Privacy and discretion are important components of menstrual hygiene and need to be a part of the puberty curriculum. For example, we don't announce to mixed company that we are wearing pads or have our period. We don't necessarily show people our pads and tampons—certainly not to boys and teachers. We can discuss our periods with girlfriends, Mom and the school nurse, but not with boys and adult males, other than perhaps our father. Understanding what's socially appropriate with regards to menstruation can be hard, and the rules can change depending upon the circumstances. We need to anticipate the various scenarios and address the social rules about menstruation, including possible exceptions to the rules, with our daughters and students. The more prepared they are for demonstrating privacy and discretion with their menstruation, the more socially appropriate they will be when they are having their periods.

It is socially appropriate for teenage girls to shave their legs and underarms. Girls who don't shave are likely to be teased and humiliated. Most neurotypical girls decide to shave on their own, but the idea of shaving may not occur to girls with Asperger's. At some point before high school, parents will need to explain the reasons for shaving and carefully instruct their daughters on leg and underarm shaving. Step-by-step instruction and practice is essential before having girls take over this task on their own.

Problem-solving can always be a challenge for students with Asperger's. Anticipate the problems they may have regarding their periods and generate appropriate solutions for them, so they will be prepared before an actual problem arises. For example, if they get their period at school and are unprepared with the necessary pads or tampons what should they do? If they accidentally stain their panties/clothing while at school, what should they do? If they develop severe cramping while away from home, what can they do? Establishing a female buddy at school who can help them out with any of these problems is always helpful, and in some cases necessary. Think about what they will need when they are away from home and how they should carry their feminine products. If your daughter doesn't have a purse or is not in the habit of carrying one, now is the time to instill the routine use of a purse.

Teaching Sex Education

Once your daughter or student is able to manage her menstrual hygiene on her own in a discreet and socially appropriate manner, then you can continue with her sex education.

I have always felt that it is important to educate students with Asperger's about sex education in high school, even though most of their neurotypical peers already know this information. By the time they reach high school, most girls with Asperger's are ready to learn about sex education, whereas earlier it may have been meaningless or too difficult to understand. As teenagers, they are typically more prepared, and mature enough, to comprehend this information. And often, given the social pressures of high school, they will need to have a thorough knowledge of sex, including sexual intercourse and other sexual acts, reproduction, sexually transmitted diseases, and birth control. Most importantly, they need to understand the rules and safety regarding dating and sex.

It actually becomes necessary to re-teach all this information to teenage girls, even if they appear to know enough about sex education. In fact, it will surprise parents and educators to know just how much about these topics teenage girls with Asperger's don't know. As a result of their naiveté, they are at a great disadvantage and can easily be persuaded to engage in sexual activities in order to gain friends, including boyfriends.

Typically, by the time girls with Asperger's are in high school, they are often more aware of their peers and usually want what everyone else wants. They want to fit in, be popular, have friends, and also have boyfriends. They don't usually know how to get a boyfriend, and, depending on how badly they want one, are often willing to do whatever it takes to have a boyfriend. Because of the nature of Asperger's girls, they can often be easily deceived and bullied into doing potentially harmful activities, including sexual acts.

Addressing Personal Safety

Issues of personal safety need to be reiterated and strongly emphasized at this time. Especially for girls, adolescence is a time of increased incidences of sexual molestation and abuse. This is especially true because they are typically not under the care of any one teacher or adult assistant at school during their adolescent years. Students are typically in more places, often unsupervised, than they were in grade school. Waiting for the bus, riding the bus, locker rooms, playgrounds, bathrooms, hallways and being out and about in the neighborhood are only some of the places where there is little or no adult supervision. Since most junior highs and high schools are large with many staff and students, usually no single adult is looking out for the best interests of a student with Asperger's. Likewise, students with Asperger's don't usually have a clique or group of friends to hang out with, who can be with them in unsupervised situations and watch their backs, so to speak. As a result, they are easy targets for bullies and anyone wishing to take advantage of them. It's no wonder that the incidence of sexual molestation for girls with special needs, including Asperger's, is 80% before the age of eighteen. (*Harvard Education Letter,* April 1999)

Girls with Asperger's tend to be immature, naïve, gullible and easily deceived. They usually want to be like others girls, and might be persuaded to do all manner of inappropriate behaviors, in order to be accepted by their neurotypical peers. Like others with Asperger's, they typically have poor problem-solving skills, and often don't know what appropriate steps to take when they are molested, abused, bullied, or taken advantage of in any way.

Physical abuse and bullying of any kind is not to be tolerated, and your daughter or student must be instructed to tell several adults, especially her parents, whenever others physically hurt her. Bullying may be more subtle, but equally frightening and troubling. Bullying can be defined as behavior towards others that is intended to intimidate, threaten, scare, tease and hurt. Bullying can often cause serious emotional, if not physical, scars. Make sure your daughter or student understands that bullying is always wrong, and the bully is the bad guy. Bullying is not a result of anything she did wrong, and is not likely to go away even if she cooperates with the bully. Sometimes school personnel do little about bullying, which is why it's important that a student always inform her parents about any bullying. Parents have the leverage to advocate for their daughter and demand a viable solution to a bullying problem.

If your daughter or student has not already learned the rules of socially appropriate touching, now is definitely the time to teach her. This information would include where it's okay to touch others, such as friends, teachers, students, and adults other than family members, as well as where it's okay for others to touch her. According to basic rules of social touching, the hands, arms, shoulders and back are generally considered okay to touch briefly in social situations. Lingering touch of any kind may cause the person who is touched to be uncomfortable and possibly upset. All other areas of the body are usually deemed inappropriate touch areas, and off-limits even for casual, social touching. It is never appropriate to touch or be touched in a person's private areas, either briefly or lingering. And this would include when a person's private areas are naked, dressed in underwear or fully covered with clothing, as in a social situation.

Hugging and kissing are also touching. Although it may have been appropriate to hug teachers and others when they were younger, as adolescents this is no longer appropriate. Kissing should be restricted to family members only, and open mouth, tongue kissing should only be allowed with long-term boyfriends or husbands.

Touching herself on her private areas, such as her breasts, buttocks and between her legs, even fully clothed, is considered a very private act and should only be done in the privacy of a bathroom stall or her own bedroom. Even if she needs to quickly adjust her panties, for instance, it is still inappropriate for her to put her hands down her pants or touch her private areas in a public place. It is always socially inappropriate to touch your private areas when others are watching. It goes without saying that if she engages in masturbation, she can only do that sexual activity in the privacy of her bedroom or bathroom when she is alone with the door shut. Furthermore, masturbating is never discussed with others, including parents, unless there is a medical problem resulting from the masturbation.

Hopefully, by the time she is an adolescent, your daughter or student should understand and demonstrate rules for modesty, and know when her privacy has been violated. It is still necessary that she demonstrate discretion and modesty when dressing and bathing, and respect the privacy of others. She needs to learn and follow the rules for changing when at school, and be suspicious of anyone who is obviously watching her, or staring at her private areas when she is undressed. It is a violation of her privacy for someone to ask to see her naked and undressed, or spy on her when she is changing. She should never allow anyone to take pictures or movies of her naked or undressing, or give pictures of herself to anyone that show her naked or undressed. This would include pictures over the internet, via email or web cam. Likewise, she should not look at or accept pictures of naked people, or people involved in various sexual acts, from others.

Make sure your daughter has a good understanding of sex, sexually transmitted diseases, and birth control long before she begins dating. Likewise, she needs to understand what constitutes sexual molestation, physical abuse and rape. Most girls with Asperger's are not knowledgeable enough or mature enough to be dating when most of their teenage peers are dating. As parents and educators, we need to be leery when our daughter or student talks about going on a date, meeting a boyfriend, talking to boyfriends online, etc. We need to find out exactly what is going on, and make very sure no one is taking advantage of her.

At some point, your daughter may decide she is ready for a sexual relationship, and if she is over the age of twenty-one, and/or living independently, there might not be much that you, as a parent or guardian, can do about it. In any case, be very sure she understands that sexual activity of any kind must be mutually consensual. She is never under any obligation to have sex with anyone, no matter what she's told. Likewise, she can decide to stop a sexual activity at any time, up to and during actual coitus. If she decides she doesn't want to continue with a sexual activity, no matter what it is, she needs to say "no" and "stop" loudly, and perhaps push her partner away. Even if her partner doesn't stop, she needs to make it very clear that she is refusing to continue.

Anytime a person (or persons) forces you to have sex, despite your protests, that is considered rape. Rape is a serious crime, which needs to be reported to the police. If your daughter is ever raped, she must immediately tell her parents or another trusted adult. Explain to her that she will need to go to the hospital to be checked by a doctor or nurse, and that the crime will then be reported to the police.

As much as we may be uncomfortable with the subject, it may be necessary for parents and therapists to help young women with Asperger's learn about dating and healthy sexual relationships. Sometimes this may involve a step-by-step instruction of what to do and say, as well as role-playing date situations. As always, we need to emphasize safety and responsibility, especially with regards to a sexually active lifestyle.

Concluding Thoughts

Adolescence can be an exciting time for kids as they grow and develop into adults, and learn more about themselves and others along the way. But it can also be a time of confusion, insecurity and loneliness. We need to do all we can as adults to help our children and students with Asperger's traverse this period in their lives. This is especially important since this is a time that will mold their personalities for many years to come.

We want our teenagers to be independent and safe. We want them to be true to themselves, and yet also be like their neurotypical peers. Parents can help their daughters fit in by learning about the appropriate fashions and hairstyles and giving their teenagers a makeover, if necessary. Sometimes it's strategic to get teen coaches and assigned "buddies" to help with that process. We need to urge our daughters and students to join clubs, organizations, and teams where they can develop friendships and explore their interests. We should encourage them to find others like themselves, by joining or forming Asperger's support groups. We need to help them to accept themselves and celebrate their strengths. Our ultimate goal, of course, is to help them become happy, safe and productive individuals as we guide them into adulthood.

The Launch:
Negotiating the Transition from High School to the Great Beyond

Meet Teresa Bolick, Ph.D.

D r. Bolick is a licensed clinical psychologist, dynamic public speaker, and author of *Asperger Syndrome and Young Children: Building Skills for the Real World*, and *Asperger Syndrome and Adolescence: Helping Preteens and Teens Get Ready for the Real World*. She earned her BA at University of North Carolina Chapel Hill, and her MA and Ph.D. at

Emory University in Georgia. She has many years of experience work-ing with children on the spectrum. She now lives in Massachusetts and consults with schools in her home state as well as in New Hampshire, where she is in private practice.

Dr. Bolick focuses on what happens as a young woman with Asperger's launches into the world. She's graduated from high school, and confi-dent that she can make it "on her own." But what happens when she leaves the nest, goes to college—and doesn't perform up to your (or her) expectations? How much "help" should you offer? And what hap-pens when she lands a job, only to discover it's not all she thought it would be?

Dr. Bolick provides commonsense answers to these questions to help young women with Asperger's and their caregivers survive this phase. She offers these encouraging words: "... almost everyone muddles through (some more gracefully than others)."

I still remember the day, though it was many years ago. When my mother dropped me off at my college dorm for the first time, I couldn't wait for her to leave. Didn't she know that I could handle this on my own? Did she think I needed her? Indeed, she finally read my signals and bid me a not-too-tearful goodbye. "This is great!" I thought. "I'm ready for anything!" My euphoria was quickly dashed when I discovered that I had left all of my "hanging clothes" at home. So much for independence! When I called to ask my mother to come down again the next day, she resisted her urge to com-ment. Looking back, I imagine that she was both relieved and amused that I still needed her. But she never voiced that "I told you so."

Many women have similar stories of their own "launch" into the world outside the confines and safety of their parents' homes. And much is made of the "failure to launch" when young adult offspring come back to the "nest" (as humorously portrayed in a recent movie). But the "launches" of young women with Asperger's Syndrome (AS) and related challenges are often much more prolonged and frustrat-ing. I'd like to share some of the trials, tribulations, and lessons learned from young women and parents whom I know.

Young Women, Parents, and "Home"

Whether we call it "launching" or "emancipation" or "empty nest," the period after high school graduation represents a young adult's opportunity to prove that she can handle life without the daily supervision and guidance afforded by parents. Making one's own decisions becomes paramount, whether the decisions are about when to go to bed, what to eat, when (or whether) to study, or what to do about friends.

When a young adult is able to move away from home during this transition, many successes and failures occur without the watchful eyes of Mom and Dad. And, while more nervous than they might want to admit, almost everyone muddles through (some more gracefully than others).

For the young woman who is not yet ready to move away from home, however, the process of independent decision-making can be more stressful. First of all, the at-home daughter can't get away with things as easily. Not that she's doing anything that bad; it's just there for all to see. Staying out too late, eating too much junk food, picking the wrong boy to date—all are there for parental scrutiny. Secondly, the "errors in judgment" then fuel the parents' anxiety that their daughter truly is not ready for the real world. Parents become more vigilant and daughters rail at the "micromanagement" (which of course fuels the parents' belief that their daughter needs more guidance). Some daughters respond to these stresses by resisting parental guidance of all kinds and angrily shutting themselves off. Others respond by "succumbing to parental wishes" (their words) and depending upon parents for all decisions. Obviously, neither of these extremes is ideal.

The young women I know have offered some advice for parents during the "launch" process:

- If you're going to encourage me to do something, you have to let me do it. Even if I make a mess in the beginning, let me follow through.
- It's okay to express your concerns, but don't get mad if I disagree.
- Work with me to set up some house rules and responsibilities. Then step back and let me follow them.

- Don't expect me to just "look around and see what needs to be done." My mind isn't on our house and family anymore; I'm thinking about my new life.

- Don't feel hurt if I don't want to hang around the house. Remember that you wanted me to learn to have a social life.

- Remember what you were like at my age.

Young Women, College, and AS

High school students with AS typically present with intellectual and academic skills that make them excellent candidates for college. Even those who have some academic gaps (such as in math) frequently find college or technical school programs that are well suited to their strengths and passions. Thus, for many young women with AS, the search for a post-high school program is quite manageable.

The difficulties emerge when it's time to go. These challenges tend to fall into three overlapping categories: self-management, academics, and relationships. In all three areas, parents and daughters can easily come into conflict. Here are a few illustrations:

Scenario #1:
Jane was scheduled to start college in the fall. She and her parents agreed that a summer school class would help her ease into the new routine. But when Jane started classes, she did not adjust her late-night bedtime. She overslept unless prodded by her parents to awaken. When she did make it to class, she fell asleep. At the end of summer school, she had a D in a class that should have been easy for her. Her parents asked, "How can we trust that you'll be able to get yourself up and to class if you're living on your own?" Jane was insulted that they did not trust her.

Scenario #2:
Maria was enrolled in a rigorous art institute. Her experience as a painter and sculptor stood her in good stead in her studio classes. Her physical and mental stamina allowed her to "do art" for many hours a day. Her challenges arose in the non-studio classes. Maria was not prepared to read and integrate fifty pages a week of art history. And her professors didn't

give out lecture notes as her high school teachers had done. Maria was "drowning" in art history by the end of the first week. When she mentioned her 504 plan to the professor, she was met with a blank stare.

Scenario #3:

Becky, her parents, and her advisor decided that a single dorm room was the best option for her freshman year at a small women's college. The single would ensure that Becky could have the quiet that she needed for studying. It would also give her a refuge from the social demands that college life entails. They also agreed that Becky should sign up for the meal plan to make sure that she spent her meal times with others. At midterms, Becky was doing well academically. She enjoyed her work-study job in the library. But she didn't know the name of anyone in her dorm. Worst of all, she stopped going to the dining hall and subsisted on ramen noodles cooked in the hot pot in her room.

In all three of these scenarios, the parents' first inclination was to rush in to help. In each case, they made well-intentioned phone calls to college personnel. And, in each case, they were told that no information could be exchanged without the student's permission. (The Family Educational Rights and Privacy Act, or FERPA, prevents schools from disclosing information without permission of the student or family. Since all three women were over 18, they "owned" their educational information and the right to disclose it or not.)

Young Women, Parents and Working Partnerships

Despite the well-intentioned parental inclination to fix, it won't work once daughters are "of age." Even if the law allowed a parent to fix things, what would that do for the ultimate goal of independence in the real world? In all three situations described above, the parents quickly realized that their best bet was to re-negotiate the terms of the "working partnerships" that they had established with their daughters earlier in adolescence. They took a step back from their natural "I will fix this" strategy to a more collaborative approach. They not only recognized their own anxiety, but they also listened carefully to their daughters' ideas about what they needed.

Scenario #1 Continued:

Jane's mother began with "What's up with you and school?" Expecting a lecture, Jane snapped, "I can handle it, Mom." Rather than giving the "Don't talk to me that way, young lady" lecture, Jane's mother took a deep breath and said, "I know you can handle it. I'm just wondering if I can help you handle it more efficiently." Over the next several weeks, Jane and her mother talked off and on about the organizational supports that had kept things on track in high school. Jane's mother let Jane experiment with her "PDA" for a week. They also tried instant messaging and email reminders and different types of alarm clocks and timers. By the beginning of fall semester, Jane was comfortable with a PDA that had built-in alarms (even reminding her to go to bed at night). Jane completed first semester with a 2.5 grade point average and much improved sleep habits!

Scenario #2 Continued:

Maria talked with her mother about the "witch" of an art history professor and tossed out strings of choice swear words. Like Jane's mother, Maria's mom resisted the urge to correct her disrespectful language. After Maria calmed down, she asked her mother what to do. Again, Maria's mother had to practice self-restraint, realizing that it wouldn't do any good for her to rush in and advise. Instead, the mother inquired about Maria's advisor as a source of assistance. Reassured that she could go to her advisor, Maria was then able to create a list of her concerns. Initially, she asked her mother to go with her to speak with the advisor. After a day or two, though, Maria decided that she could tackle this with just the advisor. Much to her surprise, the advisor agreed that this professor was a problem and that he had already taken steps to change things. The subsequent semesters continued to be challenging for Maria work-wise. But she regularly sought the assistance of her advisor and then announced the latest plans to her mother. Maria is now hard to distinguish from her classmates—exhausted, paint-covered, but passionate about her immersion in her art. (And her mother proudly pays the bills.)

Scenario #3 Continued:

Becky's parents faced greater obstacles when they tried to create a working partnership. By Becky's own admission, she was testing her parents' authority: "I didn't rebel in high school. I have to do it sometime." For months, Becky insisted on keeping to herself. She resisted going home on weekends. She stopped attending church (a serious violation of family tradition). Becky's parents disagreed about what to do. Her father maintained that Becky needed to remember that her parents were still the bosses and that they were paying the bills. Her mother hesitated to take such a rigid stand, fearing that Becky would drop out of school. After a month or so, opportunity arose. Becky needed to visit the allergist to get new prescriptions and she had no transportation. She called her mother for help. In the car, Becky began to talk about the pressures of school. She admitted that she was afraid of the social scene, because she didn't drink and she didn't want people to pressure her. She also told her mother about the social slights she had endured in high school and never revealed. After filling the prescriptions and stopping for ice cream, Becky's mother "casually" mentioned that a speech/language pathologist (SLP) whom Becky had liked in middle school was opening a practice near the college. She also told Becky that the SLP's new specialty was social pragmatics groups for young adults. Back in her dorm later that evening, Becky called her mother and asked if their insurance would pay for her to see the SLP. She also asked for the phone number. With the SLP's assistance, Becky set up a "circle of friends" at college. These young women got together with Becky once a week for a meal (not ramen noodles) and chatted about the trials and tribulations of college life. Becky was able to stay in the dorm and to complete her associate's degree. When she moved back home after college (due to low wages in her chosen field), Becky was able to be a working partner with her parents, paying room and board, helping out with cooking and housework, and going out with her friends from college.

Young Women, Parents, and Work

As tricky as college or technical school can be for young women and their parents, the world of work is often trickier. Young women and men know how to "do school." After all, they have been in school for most of their lives. But they often don't know how to negotiate the complicated world of work. Their sensory and regulatory challenges can make it difficult for them to tolerate work clothes or the workplace. Their inefficient nonverbal and verbal communication skills can interfere with every aspect of work, from the interview on. And their difficulties with organization and planning often slow productivity. For their parents, the urge to advise and fix is nearly impossible to contain!

The "simple" solution is to delegate. In other words, if your daughter is eligible for vocational supports through public agencies such as vocational rehabilitation, use your working partnership to help her apply. If she isn't eligible for public services, investigate options that may be available privately (contact your local Asperger's or autism support agencies for names). If neither of these options is available, go back to your daughter's high school and talk with their vocational counselor for ideas.

If you can't delegate the job-coaching role, use your working partnership with your daughter to set up some ground rules about how involved she needs you to be. Also, talk with her about how much to disclose to employers about her social communication and regulatory challenges. Recognize that she probably doesn't know how to approach the whole job process, other than the vague goal of "getting a job." Set up realistic goals. For example, if she is more comfortable online than in person, she probably can't go store-to-store in the mall asking for job applications. If she doesn't meet a goal, brainstorm with her about what got in her way.

And, if she gets a job, talk again about how much input she wants. Then abide by her wishes unless there is some real danger involved. A case in point: When Jane got a summer job at a local amusement park, her parents worried that her "ga-ga" approach to young children would get her fired. They were increasingly concerned when Jane came home talking about how she could just "eat up" all the darling toddlers who rode her ride that day. Tempted to give the "safe touch" lecture, Jane's mother instead asked, "Do you lift the children onto the ride?" "Oh, no!" Jane began. "That's against park rules. We are never allowed to touch the children." Jane went on to describe in great detail all of the park policies, rules that reassured her parents that they needn't worry about adequate supervision.

And, if a problem arises, remember the working partnership. As with the college student, we have to facilitate the young woman's self-advocacy rather than charging in to save the day. Listen and then ask if she would like your help.

Take-Home Tips

As parents of young adults with or without AS, we are almost constantly walking the fine line between allowing them to make their own decisions (and mistakes) and protecting them from harm. A few lessons I've learned from the parents and daughters I know:

- Ted Williams was "out" six out of every ten times he came up to bat. And no one has done better since.
- People can have fender benders and still be careful drivers.
- If she makes a mistake, it's not just because of AS.
- If we make a mistake, she'll still love us (though maybe not right at the moment).
- One child-care expert once explained that the "best" parent with the "easiest" child still makes six major parenting mistakes a day.
- The worst mistake is not trying.
- Finally, to paraphrase the Gloria Gaynor classic, "We will survive!"

Some Helpful Resources

Bolick, T. (2001). *Asperger Syndrome and Adolescence: Helping preteens and teens get ready for the real world.* Gloucester, MA: Fair Winds Press.

Grandin, T., & Duffy, K. (2004). *Developing Talents: Careers for individuals with Asperger Syndrome and high functioning autism.* Shawnee Mission, KS: Autism Asperger Publishing Co.

Harpur, J., Lawlor, M, & Fitzgerald, M. (2004). *Succeeding in College with Asperger Syndrome: A student guide.* London: Jessica Kingsley.

Meyer, R.N. (2001). *Asperger Syndrome Employment Workbook.* London: Jessica Kingsley Publishers.

Shore, S. (Ed.) (2004). *Ask and Tell: Self-advocacy and disclosure for people on the autism spectrum.* Shawnee Mission, KS: Autism Asperger Publishing Co.

online.onetcenter.org (Occupational Information Network—listing of jobs and careers, along with job descriptions, educational requirements, etc.)

Aspie Do's and Don'ts:
Dating, Relationships, and Marriage

Meet Jennifer McIlwee Myers

Jennifer McIlwee Myers is a mature, extremely intelligent, happily married woman with Asperger's Syndrome. She is also a terrific writer—funny, eloquent, and to the point. In her own inimitable way, she has gleefully (and successfully) ignored the accepted wisdom about what it takes for someone to be "happy."

Jennifer was diagnosed with Asperger's in 2002. She has a BS in Computer Science and can write a technical manual "pretty darn quick." Her interests include Disneyland, pre-1970 horror movies, Harry Potter, and rearranging her books. She often writes and speaks on autism-related topics, and lives in California with her husband Gary.

Marriage—it is not necessary that all Asperger's girls get married, no matter how stridently society claims it's the only path to bliss. "Romantic" love? Reality may be quite different from the fairy tale version. Rejection? She advises not to look at it as a "setback." Dating? Don't be fake (you can't hide your true self forever).

You will enjoy her refreshingly honest views on life, and you don't have to be an "Aspie" to benefit from them.

P lease allow me to introduce myself. I am a forty-year-old woman with Asperger's Syndrome, and I have been happily married for twelve years. Despite (or because of) all of the issues of growing up with undiagnosed AS, I've learned a lot about relationships, both from locating good research and from experience.

Mind you, I made many wrong turns and massive blunders in dating and relationships over the years. What I wish to provide for you here is the fruit of those hard-won lessons.

What the AS Girl Doesn't Need

Relationships and dating are very strange and difficult when you have AS. Dating today is an odd mish-mosh of unstructured social behaviors that involve amorphous goals and much indirect communication. Not only does this mean that dating is not an easy thing for people with AS, but also much of the long-term relationship advice available today is totally wrong for people with AS.

There are "rules" about what women need in the way of relationships that are pretty clearly communicated in our culture—so clearly communicated that most of us who have AS are bound to learn them. The problem is, these rules shouldn't be applied willy-nilly to girls with AS (and some of them shouldn't be applied to human beings in general).

Happiness Is ...?

The first of these rules about what every woman supposedly needs are:

- The best way to be happy in life is to have a long-term monogamous relationship (marriage).
- You *should* date and eventually marry.
- Any relationship is better than no relationship.

You may protest that you don't communicate all of these things to your daughter. Guess what? Even if *you* don't, the rest of the world does.

These rules deal with a massive underlying assumption that is all around us: dating is somehow *really* important, dating definitely should lead to marriage, and marriage is the best goal for everybody, especially everybody between the ages of twenty and forty. There's only one problem: it ain't necessarily so.

It is very usual for teenage girls and young women to be given tons of dating advice from a variety of sources, all of which assumes that they want to date and, if they are seventeen or older, really definitely should be dating. Not only is there lots of encouragement towards dating, but also lots of worry about girls who show no interest in it. Heaven forbid a human being be happy being single.

In the midst of all these assumptions and advice, seldom does anyone talk about what dating and relationships actually entail in terms that are realistic for girls with AS.

My sister (who has very high social skills) once asked my dad if marriage was as stressful as dating. My dad replied, "*Death* isn't as stressful as dating."

Dating is stressful, and really hard even for the socially skilled; how else would it be possible for countless books and magazines on how to date to be so profitable?

It is much easier for girls with AS to learn social skills and get to know people in more interesting and less stressful situations, like book groups and hobby-related clubs. I'll go into the details of this later, but essentially this means letting girls socialize in their own way and in their own time, without a lot of pressure to be having a specific kind of interaction with the opposite sex that involves uncomfortable small talk and itchy nylons.

Of course, it isn't just going on dates that it is the problem. It's the idea that one must seek out a member of the opposite sex for a permanent bond in order to be happy and fulfilled, and that one must do it *now* or risk lifelong misery.

This is implied so heavily and constantly that it is inescapable. If you look up "singles activities" in the weekend section of the newspaper, you'll find tons of activities that are designed for people to meet potential dates. No one goes to singles activities for the actual activity. It is as if life is a massive game of musical chairs, with everyone rushing to find a partner before the music stops.

This particular societal obsession can really hurt girls with AS. We Aspies are seldom told about some of the important questions we need to ask ourselves. These are questions like, "Do I want to date now, later, or never? Do I want someone else in my life? Would it be better to just have platonic interactions with guys until I find someone I'd really like to date? Do I want to get married in the foreseeable future? Can I deal with sharing a house with someone who might possibly touch my model airplane collection?"

Girls with AS should be encouraged from an early age to look at dating and marriage realistically, factually, and logically. The fact is if someone else is living in the same house with you, they may want to cook foods you don't like, move furniture, or otherwise do normal people things.

Simply put, it is important to start asking real questions and giving real information about relationships to girls and women with AS. Ideally, this discussion should begin before they get swept away in a surge of cultural beliefs and hormones. This may mean that parents or others need to set aside the desire to make the girl with AS more "normal" in order help her think about what is in her own best interests.

The more emotional and mercurial the girl with AS is, the more important it is to deal with these questions. The very logical, phlegmatic Aspie may well have an easier time with all of this, as the less emotional person is less likely to get caught up in the romance of romance.

Love Conquers What?

This leads me to the next set of typical "rules" about relationships that are embedded in the beliefs of our culture.

- "Falling in love" is the most important thing; the feelings associated with romantic love are more real than most things.
- You'll just *know* it when you meet The One For You.
- When you find the right person and fall in love, your life will vastly improve and your problems will disappear.

Whether we like it or not, our culture constantly communicates the idea that being in love is vital and that the feeling of being in love is really, really meaningful and important.

Take Romeo and Juliet. They meet and are devoutly in love before either of them knows anything about the other; they essentially have no actual relationship, but rather a series of "stolen time" encounters; and they quite stupidly hide what is going on in strange ways and wind up killing themselves like the dumb, hormone-riddled, immature twits they are. And they are our culture's ideal of love. Geesh.

The vast majority of people in our culture seek out romantic love quite desperately, which is no surprise when the vast majority of pop songs, TV shows, and movies are focused on the joys and supposedly sublime sorrows of the damn stuff.

The fact is, romantic love has many attractive points, not the least of which is that it is the emotional equivalent of crack. It has a bio-chemical kick that is quite powerful.

Most parents don't talk to their children about the fickle and unreliable aspect of romantic love until said children actually fall in love. Many times, the talks that follow are about how the child is too young to really be in love, and how unsuitable the other young person is. For some reason, even now parents still haven't noticed that this kind of talk leads nowhere good. Whether the child has AS or not, you might as well dip yourself in steak sauce and walk onto the turf of a hungry pride of lions.

Girls with AS, particularly the mercurial ones like myself, are extra vulnerable. Overwhelming cultural messages, which are communicated verbally, visually, and in music—thus, in every possible way a person with AS might learn best—can leave us more naïvely sure of the importance of love than even our typical peers (who are nuts on the subject).

One should appeal to a girl's intellect and capacity for reasoning before actual romance is on the horizon. The simple fact that it is completely possible to fall deeply, madly in love with someone who should be avoided at all costs should be mentioned. The fact that it is completely possible but really hard to make head-based decisions when one is overwhelmed by the biochemistry of love should be explained.

Perhaps even more importantly, girls with AS should know that romantic love is not necessary to human happiness and it is okay not to feel it. This is another case in which it is vital for girls to understand that they don't have to fit the mold, and that falling in love is not the all-purpose cure-all that it is widely cracked up to be.

As an Aspie who has both conditions, I can assure you that being in love and having special interests (aka "autistic obsessions") are much the same feeling. However, being in love involves another human being, who has free will, while an obsession with, say, trains, usually does not.

Trains and other objects of special interests are reliable. Once you decide that you are devoted to building and improving your train set, the train set does not look at you like you're nuts or wonder where you ever got that idea. Model airplanes do not decide that they want to be built by someone else who is more attractive or less needy.

It is important that girls with AS understand this: no matter how you feel about someone, their feelings may not be the same, and that fact *is no reflection on you*. The one you have become attached to may be much less intelligent and discerning than you think, or may just not be interested. The simple fact is that getting rejected is part of life. The level on which this sucks defies the laws of physics, but there it is.

For some reason, this is more difficult for those of us with AS than it is for the typical folks around us. Maybe it has to do with the whole "theory of mind" thing. Maybe it is because we hyper-focus on one goal to an extent that others don't.

From my own experience, I would say that the best way for a mercurial/emotional female with AS to deal with rejection is two-fold.

One, always be aware that rejection is not a real setback. If I approached a guy I was interested in and got rejected, then in fact I was no worse off than I was before I approached. If I thought I had a good relationship with a guy and then he dumped me, then that really good relationship existed only in my mind, not in the real world. If the relationship existed only in my head, there was in fact no relationship; once rejection occurs, it merely means that I have been informed of that fact. The situation has not actually deteriorated. This is really, really important. Understanding that the loss of a one-sided fantasy is not the loss of a reality or potential reality is vital.

Two, I use a somewhat cognitive-behavioral approach to deal with the depression and general crankiness that can follow rejection. That is, I drag myself through the standard tasks of life. I'm going to be miserable if I try to go through my daily routine, but I'm going to be just as miserable if I don't, so I might as well keep going. This is important, as it is not unusual for a depressed Aspie going through a bad rejection to fail to do basic, necessary things and wind up in a genuinely bad situation, such as being in trouble at work or flunking a class due to too many cuts.

Once again, the best tools that a girl with AS has are logic and facts.

The Suitable Partner

The next rule is one most folks don't realize they devoutly believe in.

- There are certain types of people you should date and who you are best off marrying. Those people should match your own demographic quite closely.

This "rule," or myth, is not nearly so dangerous to the Aspie directly as it can be hurtful to her through those around her.

While often we'd like to think that we, as a civilization, do not judge people on race, creed, color, age, or social class, when it comes to dating, we do. The range of ages, colors, and other variables that are acceptable in a long-term mate are generally pretty narrow.

This rule, or set of rules, is so ingrained that when it comes to dating, most people won't take a second look at someone who doesn't fit their demographic range.

Our society is rather obsessive about this; every time a famous woman dates a man who isn't within a few years of her age, there are dozens of TV and entertainment-magazine articles. If the man is more than a few years her senior, the stories are scandalized; if the man is her junior, the stories are exaggerated "you go girl" applause. Either way, the message is clear: being with someone who doesn't "fit" you makes the relationship the equivalent of a freak show.

In fact, as late as 1967, thirty-eight of the United States of America had laws on the books that made intermarriage of whites with any non-white illegal. Nowadays, we have people who bend over backwards to show how okay it is with them when people of different races marry—once again calling attention to how strange something is with loud and over-done noises of acceptance.

Girls (and guys) with AS are not nearly so likely to take these societal restrictions into account. Many of us lack the social awareness and social skills to efficiently pre-judge people by category. We are just more likely to date and marry people who don't fit the standard. If the people around us can be accepting of this, the situation is unlikely to be any worse than any other dating or marriage relationship. It may be better, as it may well be based on internal qualities more than external qualities.

My own husband is just thirteen years my senior (not the biggest age gap you'll find by a long shot). Many people have seen fit to assure me that the gap is no big deal without me asking.

Fortunately for me, my parents had a pact that they made when I was very little. They promised each other that they would not say anything negative about anyone their children dated or married. They knew that such comments divided families and drove many people to become more attached to the guy (or girl) their parents disapproved of.

After all, if you have to defend your boyfriend to your parents all of the time, you are constantly thinking about how great his strengths are and how small his flaws are by comparison. He looks better and better the more they attack him. It creates an us-against-them mentality, as well. Parental disapproval is excellent glue that can cement a relationship quite solidly.

Thus, the first time my dad met my husband Gary, who is closer to my dad's age than mine, he made no negative comments to me, even though I think he was a little thrown by the age gap. The reason I think so is that Dad said to me, no less than five separate times, "Well, he seems to be very … mature."

Dad was trying so hard to say something nice he kind of gave himself away, but I knew about the pact and also that Dad would get used to Gary. Now Dad thinks I've got a really great husband and says lots of nice things about him.

I'll always appreciate the fact that when Dad was thrown off my the age difference, the only thing he said was, "He seems very mature." To me, those words were the sound of the dad who really, really loves me, even if I don't stay within my own demographic.

Appearances Count, But How?

The next three myths are variations on a theme:

- The way to get yourself a man is to be feminine or dress in a certain way.
- Act like the kind of person that guys want and you'll get a guy.
- Men are afraid of smart women who speak their minds.

These rules are fabulously commonly believed. What one wears on the first date is considered to be of tremendous interest; hiding certain personal traits is considered to be par for the course. I'm not just talking about putting one's best foot forward; this often involves taking on an essentially false persona.

Fortunately a fairly large number of girls with AS just aren't comfortable being fake; they may dress up in Star Trek uniforms for conventions, but they'll be hanged if they'll wear nylons for a date.

The reality is that parents and friends will often give dubious advice along these lines in the hope of "softening" a girl with AS. The reality is no matter how well intended this advice is, it's like setting a time bomb.

You see, no one can be fake forever. No one can hide her true self while wearing itchy, impractical clothes forever. At some point reality will kick in. Oh, will it ever!

Don't try to change a girl with AS in order to help her get a date. Work with her within her own comfort zone, and don't worry that this means that guys looking for a more standard model will pass her by.

A man who is put off by bluntness will simply not be able to deal with an Aspie long-term. A person to whom a specific kind of appearance is vital is not going to be able to cope with a woman whose dress-sense must take into account both sensory issues and an inordinate amount of time spent in hobbies such as, say, feral cat capture-spay/neuter-release programs or anything involving horses.

For me, being guy-bait just never happened. After I had been married to Gary for some years, I was talking to a good friend (a research psychologist with a strong interest in relationship psychology). I mentioned that while pictures from my teens and twenties showed I was pretty cute, somehow I'd never attracted many guys, while my (no-less-adorable) kid sister had to beat them off with a stick.

My friend replied, "Jenn, you do beat them off with a stick!"

She went on to explain that my attitude toward guys in general involved challenging them in "guy" areas, such as computers, and basically meeting them much more on a guy level than a feminine one. She told me that my behaviors were a giant signal to any guy who might be interested to BACK OFF.

I did find this information useful, not because I wanted to attract guys, but because I wanted to be less off-putting and more approachable to other humans when it was appropriate to be so.

More importantly, when this conversation took place, not only had I been happily married for several years, but also this same research psychologist had asked me for relationship advice several times. She felt I had one of the best marriages she'd ever seen.

Popular beliefs that encourage you to hide your true self really are just myths. You don't find your one true love by being fake; you find him by living your life and being the best version of you that you can achieve. A girl or woman with AS isn't going to find her best life by trying to be neurotypical, but rather by striving to be the best darn Aspie she is able to be.

The advantage of this is that if you try to be your best YOU, you have permanent benefits that will last all of your life, whether you are alone, married, or in-between. The Aspie who is taught to be someone she can't really be won't have permanent benefits, but rather permanent stress.

Where Is the Love?

Where to find love is a matter of much conjecture, but most people seem to start in the areas indicated by the next two rules.

- Opposites attract.
- Heavily social places and events are good places to meet people.

We have a society that believes both that "birds of a feather flock together" and that "opposites attract." The fact is that massive amounts of data tell us that people who have much in common are most likely to get along and feel they have a good relationship from date one straight through to late in marriage.

Girls with AS, even more than boys with AS, are often bombarded with variations on the idea that being more social and being a better person are the same. Females in our society are expected to be the social glue that holds families and pretty much every social group together. The anthropologists and social psychologists call a lot of this kin keeping, and females are the kin keepers.

Thus the pressure to be sociable is even greater for girls with AS than for boys. The pressure is pretty heavy on most kids with AS; the reasoning seems to be that if someone has a "disability" that makes them less interested in social activities, the "cure" is to make them be more social. (This seems to me much like curing broken legs through a regimen of jogging.)

The message sent is social=good, anti-social or asocial=bad. People with strong social skills are presented as being just plain better.

In the dating world, many of the standard places people go hunting are social realms, such as dance clubs, bars, and parties. A large fellowship group or other large faith-related social occasion is supposed to be ideal. If social=good, then looking for a fellow in these places is good, right?

Not really. It is nearly impossible to get to know people in places that are sensory nightmares, even for the neurotypicals. And the people who shine under those circumstances, the ones we are most likely to notice, are the highly sociable types.

After all those years of being pushed to imitate and hang out with the most sociable and socially skilled kids at school, many girls with AS will pick out just such people at social events. We're just following a pattern we've been taught. For us most social occasions are something we do because we have to or because we've been told that we ought to. For the fellows who thrive in those places, social occasions are the best thing ever. See a problem coming? I thought you would.

Dating (or, heaven forbid, marrying) a fellow with a high level of social interests and needs can put a girl with AS in quite a pickle. She is trying to be good by following the rules about socializing that have been pounded into her head, but the actual social situations are stressful outings that involve both constant alertness and careful mimicry of others' behaviors.

After a night out or group outing, an Aspie can be very drained and will need quite a bit of alone time for recovery. Meanwhile, Mr. Wonderful has been recharged through social interaction, and is ready to invite the gang over for pizza and a movie.

Aspie girls need solitude for recharging and for processing what has happened that day, as well as for general thinking and just for the pleasure of it. Sociables often find solitude irksome and will try to remedy or prevent it.

You see, the "empathy" thing works both ways. We have difficulty empathizing with sociables; they have just as much trouble empathizing with us. A sociable guy will *know* that solitude is boring and draining, and try to rescue his Aspie gal-pal from it.

The well-trained girl with AS, who has been taught that more sociable is *better*, may well try to go along with this, and strain herself to the brink of snapping. Or even go past the brink.

When that snap happens, watch out! A girl or woman with AS who has been sociable when she needed solitude is not going to mince words. The word "meltdown" does not do it justice. A person who is strained to her utmost ability to cope and then asked to do just a little more will have plenty of rage and no emotional resources for recovery. It's not a pretty thing.

This isn't just a dating and relationship issue, of course. Well-meaning parents and teachers can strain a girl with AS in the same way if they don't understand the value of solitude and the stress of the social world. When romantic hopes and feelings are added to the mix, it can make for much more pain.

A girl with AS who wants to date the "right" kind of guy (can you say, "rule bound?") and get both his and her family's approval may do her best to patch it up with the fellow and go back to trying to fit his social whirl. The result can be a vicious cycle that will only end with a sad and ugly break-up.

What's really sad is that the above is a best-case scenario. The reality is that there are two much more likely results for girls with AS who are pushed to go out to clubs and parties to try to meet guys.

One likely scenario is that girls (or guys) with AS will wind up being wall-flowers and going home empty handed. That bald statement doesn't quite express what the experience is like. Going on your own, milling around trying to find someone or some group that will let you join in, and then going home on your own adds up to real misery.

Being in a situation where one is judged purely on outer appearances and social finesse is not a good idea for girls with AS or other human beings.

The other most-likely scenario is sadly common. When a girl with a low level of social skills and/or a poor ability to read people goes to a highly social scene, she will stand out to the users in the crowd. The harder she is trying to meet people, the more she will stand out as a target. The vic-timizers, as well as the careless narcissists, will often pick her out.

Guys with great social skills who *use* women—for sex, for loans they'll never pay back, or for sheer ego-boost—exist in every club, party, and bar. The fellow who knows all the right things to say and can stay up talking romantic nonsense all night in order to get that cash loan will be around. Avoiding social hot spots is a good way to get to know as few of these guys as possible.

That last section begs the question: how can I say at one point that girls with AS are likely to be attracted to guys regardless of social boundaries and at another that girls with AS are likely to be attracted to the kind of guy they have been taught is the "right" kind?

The reality is that the treatment and education that girls with AS get is very different from case to case. A girl who has an accepting family and who gets support from professionals who respect who she is will not be tightly bound by societal rules of who to date. A girl who is pushed to be the sociable, "normal" girl that she really can't be will learn a lot of rules that are contrary to who she is and will cause her great pain as her "rule bound" Aspie nature ties her up in others' expectations.

What the AS Girl DOES Need

Now that I've gone through the things that *don't* work, there is an important question to address—exactly what is a girl with AS, or parent who wants to help, supposed to do about relationships and dating?

There are three main points that are of importance here: first, that not being "normal" is just fine; second, that the most important relationship skills are actually friendship skills; and third, that when it comes to the basic facts and problems of sex, ignorance is a very bad thing.

One thing I deeply wish that I'd learned much sooner is that "normal" isn't necessarily "best" or even all that good. I don't mean any insult to neurotypicals, or to normal people, whoever they may be. It's just that normalcy doesn't equal happiness, while struggling for a false image of normalcy usually equals unhappiness.

I have had many opportunities to talk to parents of teens and pre-teens with AS, and the questions they most want an answer to is, "How can I make my child socially adept? How can I get her to want to be sociable like the other kids?"

The answer is, of course, you can't. The more important answer is you *shouldn't*. Girls with AS need more time to recover from social interactions than typical girls, and they must work harder in social situations than typical girls. Trust me, even when I am in a social situation I've learned to deal with well, and it looks like I'm just blending in, it's a huge effort. That doesn't mean I never have fun in a social situation; it just means that I need less time socializing and more time recovering in order to manage. You can have fun hiking all day, but there is a limit to how much hiking a body can stand.

Frankly, this whole socializing for socializing's sake thing that neurotypicals do is rather unappealing and fairly incomprehensible. It's even more puzzling than chewing tobacco; at least one can understand that some people like to ingest stimulants in various forms. Why some folks will go out to dinner with friends the same day they've attended an *entire* baby shower is a mystery to me, and to a lot of my Aspie sisters.

Yes, we with AS do jump at the chance to join a social group from time to time. After all, no one wants to be totally left out.

The pressure from one or more family members to be "like the other kids," and get involved with a social group, any social group, can make a girl desperate to find a way to stop the nagging and put-downs. The thousandth time a girl hears, "Why don't you just *try* to make friends?" she will feel pretty low. Even outside of the dating world, this can have a negative effect. You see, the easiest ways to fulfill outside pressure to be sociable are the worst ways to be sociable.

The easiest way for a teenage girl to be more popular and have more people to hang out with is for her to do the exact things no caring person would want her to do, such as drinking, smoking, and sleeping around indiscriminately. It's much better to be a bit of a loner than to get tangled up with kids who show their group loyalty and identity by hanging outside the liquor store trying to talk adults into buying them booze.

The same goes for adults, unfortunately. The easiest way to find a lot of "friends" fast is to be more or less self-destructive, and to run up credit-card debt buying rounds. The easiest way to get married fast is to stop being fussy and settle for a guy who is just using you.

Sadly, a girl (or boy, or woman, or man) with AS who is being shoved into social situations will know, for sure, that the person who is pushing her that way does not accept her for who she is, nor want what is actually best for her. What makes a neurologically-typical parent, grandparent, or sibling happy and fulfilled is not going to be healthy or helpful for a girl with AS.

So can a girl or woman with AS find and develop a long-term (or short term) romantic relationship? She certainly can, if that is what *she* wants.

As you might have guessed by now, those of us who are females with AS often need to approach developing the social skills for dating and relationships in ways that are a bit "different." But we still can benefit from advice and support from parents and other family members.

Do we need some kinds of advice and information? Yes. Oh, heck, yes! Factual information about typical guy and girl dating behavior can save us a lot of grief. Girls with AS need lots of factual information, rationally put, about everything from how to turn down a date to the fact that each of us is in charge of her own body and should never have to compromise that.

Factual information about typicals? Yes, please. Typical expectations? Not so much.

Relationships Skills for Girls with AS

The most important skills for dealing with relationships have little to do with the traditional idea of "what to do on a date." The single most important set of relationship skills are, in fact, friendship skills.

Many girls with AS have trouble developing basic friendship skills: the give-and-take of mutual conversation, the issue of being clean and neat so as not to stink, and other basics often elude us. The main reason we don't develop friendship skills is that we don't develop friendships. The main reason we don't develop friendships is that we spend most of our childhoods exposed only to people we can't make friends with.

The reality is that most typical peers, especially from ages five to twenty, are not suited to Aspie friendship. These typical kids go through an assorted set of rapidly discarded social skills and expectations—skills that change every few months, so that what was completely cool for the kids who were three months into sixth grade is totally geeky for kids who are five months into sixth grade. This goes on for at least one and a half decades of life!

The best basis for friendship is common interests. The best basis for marriage is a solid base of common interests, values, and a shared idea of what married life should be like. Knowing this, take a guess: how likely is it that a teen with AS is going to find someone they can have an actual relationship with who fits the NT profile of an appropriate friend or partner?

The answer is just about nil. The good news is that there are a lot of grown-up people out there, both male and female, who share the kinds of interests and ideas of fun that we Aspies have. They are usually called "geeks."

So where does the girl with AS meet people?

She meets them in common interest groups. There are dozens of science-fiction book clubs, model train clubs, chess societies, Sherlock Holmes reader societies, Scrabble® clubs, and other groups of dedicated geeks, wonks and nerds all over the place.

While internet dating is fraught with peril, the internet is a good place to find groups that meet in the real world. Enter the kind of special interest and your location into any decent search engine and you have a good chance of finding something.

Common special interests are the most important social tool and basis for social contacts among Aspies. Read that again. And again. And again. Okay, now you can stop and go on.

You may not feel your daughter's dream man should speak fluent Klingon, but she may be happiest if they write their own vows in it. For other girls with AS, what matters most is size—the size of a fellow's Lego® model train layout, that is. And some girls will go ga-ga over a guy who has been on every major wooden roller coaster east of the Mississippi.

Even if your daughter's special interest is focused around *Pride and Prejudice*, and the local Jane Austen club is a little short on available men, it's a great way to get social. Friendship skills *are* relationship skills.

If the local model train club consists entirely of happily married old fellows, that will still provide the Aspie girl with a chance to develop friendships so that she learns to relate to other people. Even a ten-year-old with AS is more likely to make friends at such a group than at school.

And everyone in that model train club, Jane Austin book club, or other group will also have a family and friends. They have brothers, sons, grandsons, or nephews. The grandson of a model railroad buff or other special-interest geek is more likely than average to be "AS friendly"; he's been programmed by genetics and upbringing either to be one or to live with them!

No special interest groups around? There is another opportunity no girl with AS should miss: volunteering!

When I was in my early teens, my mother got good and sick of having me mope at home all summer. She did a little research and found that I was old enough for the summer volunteer program at a local nursing home. She knew that particular home very well, as my grandfather volunteered there often.

At the nursing home, *everyone* was happy to see me—it was like the opposite of school. The residents liked having someone to talk to, and the nurses liked the fact that the volunteers raised the morale of the residents. My special interests of Fred Astaire movies and old-time radio shows were of much greater interest to people at the home than to any typical peer.

Just as good was the fact that I got clear but kind feedback from the volunteer supervisor, so I knew when I made social errors and got helpful suggestions to correct them. It was so great that I did it for several summers, and put in more hours than any other teen volunteer!

Trust me, you learn a lot about relationships in a nursing home. Many women there had pictures of themselves with their late husbands as young people, and many women missed their late husbands sorely. They would have gladly put up with all the snoring and golf talk in the world to have that special fellow back for another day. When you come face to face with the fact that life is short and some things just aren't so important in the long run, it sticks with you.

Talk About It

These friendship/relationship skills are something that typical folks don't need to be told about, but we with AS do. Girls with AS need to be told out loud about how to use these chances for developing skills, and that these skills apply in more than one place.

Tell your daughter, *out loud*, that when you learn to interact with one person, you learn important things about interacting with humans in general.

My parents were, thank heavens, very good at teaching me how to learn from observing people. This is the reason I didn't repeat the same stupid relationship mistakes more than five or six times each. That may seem like a lot, but it seems that most people make those same mistakes over and over their whole lives.

My mom made it clear that dating wasn't what the women's magazines thought it was. She must have told me dozens of times, "Dating isn't about finding Mr. Right. Dating is about interacting with a variety of people and finding out what you do and don't like about them. You can only learn what you like and what you can't stand if you interact with people and pay attention to your own feelings and to how they react to you."

She also told me, "Your male relatives are key to figuring out what you need in a relationship. You interact with your dad, Pop-pops and uncles often over a long period of time, which gives you a chance to figure out what traits in guys you can live with, what you really can't live with, and what makes you feel happy to spend time with someone."

It took me a long and roundabout route to get where I am today, but these facts, frequently stated by my mother, made it less circuitous and much less painful than it might have been. You can't prevent all mistakes and you can't save your child from every heartache, but you can give them a push in the right direction.

Of course, there is another area of knowledge that girls with AS need crystal clear information on.

Let's Talk About Sex (Heaven Help Us)

Talking about relationships means the issue of sex is nearby. For girls with AS, ignorance about sex means social problems, vulnerability, and a harder time with relationships later in life.

There is a tremendous amount of adult denial about the ages at which children become aware of the topics connected to sex. Let's start with an example from my own life.

My sister and I were quite well sheltered. My parents didn't even let us watch *The Producers* or *A Funny Thing Happened on the Way to the Forum* before we were eighteen; they loved those movies, but we were banished to our rooms every time they were on lest we see something inappropriate. That's right; the edited-for-broadcast versions of those films were not tame enough for us to see. However, parents do not constitute a child's whole life.

When I was eleven, all of the kids in my class watched *Soap*, but I didn't, because my parents felt I was too young. I did a lot of begging and pleading, as all of the other kids were talking about the show and I was left out and laughed at because I wasn't allowed to see it.

Finally, in the second season, when I was twelve, my folks decided I could watch the show with them (at least a few times). The first time we watched, I was totally excited. I sat on the floor watching with great focus.

Meanwhile, my younger sister, Catherine, who was eight at the time, came into the room to ask my parents a question. My dad answered quickly, nervous because my sister might see a show that was blatantly inappropriate for her.

After he answered her question, just as she was turning to leave, something on the TV caught her eye and she asked, "Why is that guy talking to that other guy like that?"

My folks looked at each other, and my dad opened his mouth a few times without speaking. Finally, he said, "Jenn, can you explain this to your sister?"

I turned to her and said, "He's gay, Cath," and went back to watching the show. Cath said, "Oh," and left the room.

My parents were stunned, totally stunned, especially my dad. How could his eight-year-old daughter "get" such an answer? And she was so calm about it, as if she'd always known.

The things that a typical eight-year-old like my sister was comfortable discussing with other girls were simply far and away beyond what my parents dreamed. And this was in 1978, when having a gay character in prime time was a big honkin' deal, and would never have been allowed before 9:30pm.

The reality is that typical children often hear and talk about sex and related topics quite young. Once a typical child is over seven, the vast majority of his or her social interactions with other kids are totally hidden from adults. Please don't think your child's school is different because it is private, or religious, or in a small town. Kids talk about sex. If you're ten, knowing a dirty joke is worth a world of "street cred" on the playground!

A young girl with AS is likely be bombarded with sexual information that she doesn't quite know how to parse, and may well overhear lots of stuff as other kids talk at school, when the teacher isn't around.

Most importantly, girls with AS are likely to pick up less coherent information about sex than other children. Their comparative ignorance will not only provide extra fodder for bullying and teasing, but it can also make them a target for sexual harassment from other kids or even adults.

The comparative ignorance situation only gets worse with time. A lot of girls, especially AS girls, start puberty earlier than you'd expect. I reached my full growth, height and all, before I turned thirteen.

If a girl with AS isn't even aware of the possibility of puberty, the results can be extra painful. Remember *Carrie*? Don't think for one instant that kids aren't capable of extreme cruelty in real life.

I understand that many people feel it is appropriate, even necessary, for parents to protect their children's "innocence" by strictly limiting information about sex. The problem with that is that ignorance and innocence are not at all the same thing.

A lot of those people think it's good to teach even very young children about the difference between appropriate use of medications and illicit drug use, because they want to protect those children from harm. Those same folks are often afraid that information about sex will turn their daughters into wild girls.

The truth is, plenty of accurate information is not dangerous. Ignorance is.

When I was twelve, I obtained access to a copy of *The Joy of Sex*. I immediately read it several times through. While it is not the kind of book most people would recommend for a young teen, it was actually pretty good. It was factual, it was straightforward, and it was even oriented towards committed couples. Reading it thoroughly definitely didn't turn me into a teen sex maniac. It wasn't until many years later that I so much as kissed a guy. Knowledge about sex just does not equal going out and doing it.

Mind you, if I'd had access to good books on sex that were aimed at my age and developmental level, I wouldn't have been hunting all over for decent information. It also would have saved me a lot of time and bother reading those darn Judy Bloom books; I hate chick lit, but Bloom put clear and simple information about puberty into some of her work, so I slogged through those soggy, girly books repeatedly. I wanted the information.

Alas, my parents had only offered us only one book: *The Wonderful Story of How You Were Born*. Blech. When I was as young as six, I was frustrated by the fact that the book was deliberately, mind-bogglingly vague. Since my parents had picked this book out and brought it out in answer to any questions on the subject, I inferred that they simply weren't going to tell me anything.

Of course my parents wanted to be helpful and informative, and they wanted me to come to them first with my questions. They had no idea how clearly they communicated the opposite of what they wanted to say.

That's right; even a girl with AS who has little social awareness can pick up on those none-too-subtle signals from parents that while they want their children to feel free to ask them anything, they really aren't clear on what to say and don't really want to give actual information.

When a girl has to hunt for information herself, that's a problem for obvious reasons. Less obvious is the fact that when a girl doesn't have the curiosity that would lead to such hunting, that is just as big a problem. Not knowing what is going on can get you into bad situations.

If a girl is nine or older (yes, nine!), she should have two or three books addressing the topics of sex and puberty that are at her reading level. This means both the curious and not-curious girl will have basic, clear information in a non-social context. (Talking with your parents is a social inter-action. Social interactions are problematic for people with AS. 'Nuff said.)

When I say books, I mean books that say the things you are embarrassed to say directly. They should even have drawings of the dreaded dangly bits. I would strongly suggest, at a minimum, *Where Did I Come From?* by Peter Mayle, *What's Happening to Me?* also by Mayle, and *The Care and Keeping of You: The Body Book for Girls* from the American Girl Library. That's an absolute dead minimum, but it's a start.

The reason for using books is simple: even those of us with AS who are linguistically fluent can have great difficulty framing questions and having actual conversations about difficult topics. The "sex talk" as usually given is about as helpful to us as road signs written in cuneiform (except, of course, for those Aspies who have a special interest in cuneiform).

I remember when my dad decided it was time to have a "man to man" talk with my younger brother, who has autism. Dad started out by saying, "Well, soon you'll become a man." Jimmy replied, "I don't want to be a man. I want to stay a little boy forever." Then he wouldn't listen to a single thing my dad had to say!

The fact is that most people address this topic in a non-literal and very confusing way. This means that girls with AS are likely to be confused and not know what to ask. Worse, they may be confused and misunderstand things badly, but not know it!

Books (with pictures!) are much more useful. They don't try to make eye contact, they don't fuss about our stimming or mannerisms, and they aren't likely to be embarrassed. They are the same every time you go to them. They are ideal teachers for this topic.

When a girl with AS has never read simple, accurate information about what the heck sex is, she's very vulnerable. Her own body can easily become a confusing mystery, to start with. Then there is always a fellow out there who will act as if he'd just invented some activity as a substitute for "real" sex. It doesn't really count, he'll say, and he'll also tell her it's totally safe and would prove she really does care about him after all. She really, really, REALLY needs to know that, yes, oral sex has been around for awhile, that, yes, there are guys who will try to talk her into it with little regard for her feelings, and yes, people do get STDs from it.

All girls with AS need to be told, frequently, that their bodies are under their own jurisdiction, and no one else's. All those years of everyone putting "compliance" as a goal on their IEPs can backfire badly if they aren't told they have the absolute, irrevocable right to say no! They also should be told that if a guy is pushy, there is no need to be polite. Saying, "Scram!" is just fine.

But, you say, my daughter is very innocent and sheltered and only socializes with the church youth group. *Get her the darn books!*

When parents give an Aspie girl incomplete and therefore only half-right information, deliberately leaving things out they find embarrassing or inappropriate, they run a serious risk. We with AS are very sensitive about honesty. As soon as we find out that someone gave us information that was only part of the truth, we lose our trust in that person.

At the same time, it doesn't matter how sheltered a girl with AS is, or how many times you work on pounding the idea of abstinence into her head. First of all, she is going to go through puberty and has to deal with hormones no matter what. You can't stop that.

Secondly, if a girl with AS socializes with any teenage males of any sort, there is a good chance that the predators of the group will spot her right away.

Just as those of us with ASDs seem to have an invisible target on us that every con artist in the world can see, girls with AS are targets for guys who want a vulnerable girl whom they can manipulate easily.

Simply having a popular guy pay attention to her is a big deal for a girl with AS. The pressure to be socially accepted is tremendous for many girls with AS. In short, we're sitting ducks.

No group of teens, no matter how clean cut, is wolf-proof. There are both guys and girls out there with the social savvy to seem like ideal teens to the adults while being quite different just outside of the adults' range of vision. See myspace.com for details.

How I Did It

After telling you about all of these concerns, caveats, and pitfalls, I should mention that it is possible to get through it all and have a happy, healthy life, with or without a partner. I did, and others can, too.

I was fortunate enough to have parents who did not feel I had to be normal to be successful, to find decent information on puberty and sex early on, and to have been taught how to use mistakes and bad experiences as learning tools. I was unfortunate enough to absorb a lot of misinformation and to try far too hard to fulfill what I perceived as the right way to find a fellow. I dearly wish I had been told that most of what our society tells us about relationships just wouldn't fit me.

When I was a young woman, much of what I knew about dating and marriage came from reading as much about the topics as possible and listening to other females discuss those topics.

You see, it's very important to me to find out the correct rules for doing things and then to do those things correctly. Thus, I spent a lot of time figuring out what I "should" look for in a guy according to people who seemed to be experts.

I tried very hard to learn and follow the rules for dating and finding a husband. I married someone who fit everyone's idea of the perfect guy for me when I was not quite twenty-one. We split up just five years later, but those five years each felt like a century. We were deeply, fundamentally unsuited for each other.

Fortunately, that experience was enough to snap me about of my belief that listening to other people was a good way to find the correct rules. When I stopped listening to the external pressures to do dating a certain way, things got a lot better.

I got together with a guy who had been a platonic friend for a long time. We met in a science-fiction and fantasy book discussion group (not the kind of place you're supposed to find Mr. Right). He is, as I said, older than I am by thirteen (and a half) years. He was forty and had dated three, count them, THREE women in his entire life, none before he was twenty-six years old. He lived quietly with his books in an apartment done entirely in shades of brown. His spare time was spent adding to his collection of first editions of great twentieth-century fantasists, a collection started when he was twelve, or else writing Lovecraftian pastiches.

He was too old, too anti-social, and it was too soon after I'd left my husband. It was all wrong by so many of the rules I'd been taught, but he was a real friend and let things go at my pace, not his. He never pushed, never was aggressive, and treated me like I was the greatest human being ever.

Now we've been married for thirteen-plus years. During my first marriage, I dropped out of college. During this one, my husband gave me all the support I needed to go back and get my degree in computer science. When I started talking and writing about autism, my husband backed me to the hilt, and has ever since. His apartment is no longer all brown and sedate; I'm afraid I've added a lot of chaos and color to his life.

What I needed was NOT to date by the usual rules. I needed to date according to the kind of person who I would actually want to spend a lot of time with and who would be happy spending a lot of time with me. Yes, I know that statistically speaking, I'll likely outlive him by twenty years, which sucks, but it's worth it.

My goal here has been to convince you that there are "rules" that girls with AS do need to know and be taught, such as the importance of using your head as well as your heart in matters of romance, and the fact that just because everyone in our culture knows that romantic love is the most important thing in the world doesn't mean it actually is. There are also rules they don't need to know, and I've told you why.

Girls and women with AS can survive and thrive in a society that is obsessed with relationships. The best thing you can do for a girl with AS is to accept that she has AS and work from there.

In Conclusion

As it is with so many areas of life, what girls with AS need to have successful relationships and to cope with the world's addiction to sex and dating is *knowledge*. They need to be given the knowledge that who they are is okay and they don't have to conform to others' ideas about popularity, dating, and finding relationships. They need to develop knowledge of friendship skills through Aspie-friendly social interactions. They need a clear knowledge of puberty and sex so they can take care of their own bodies and make their own decisions about what they will and won't do.

Parents, teachers, and professionals can all help girls and women with AS develop these kinds of knowledge. Starting early on is best, but for older girls and women with AS, starting right now is just fine.

The sooner the learning process starts, the sooner the knowledge base is developed, the more fulfilling life can be for someone who has the knowledge and skills to make her own decisions about relationships and pursue her own goals.

As for me, I need to go ask my husband to dust his Universal Monsters action figures, and then I'm going to decide where to put the lovely bust of Boris Karloff he gave me. Life is good.

Maternal Instincts in Asperger's Syndrome

Meet Ruth Snyder

Ruth Snyder is a Registered Nurse and a single mom of four great kids, two of whom have been diagnosed with autism. She was diagnosed with autism as an adult, though she didn't understand what it meant for a long time. But she hasn't let that stop her. She has almost completed her BSN, and plans to study neuroscience or become a Registered Nurse Anesthesiologist in the future.

Ms. Snyder also loves to write, and hopes to have more of her work published. Another goal is to become a positive role model, public speaker and advocate for others on the spectrum. She's accomplished several of those goals with the publication of this article.

Ruth Snyder's story is often painful to read, as she describes a childhood of abuse and neglect. The expression of her experiences is as significant as their content; hers is a genuine voice from the world of autism.

She's survived many betrayals—by uncaring parents who were ashamed of her; lovers who used her and left her; doctors who misdiagnosed her and her children; and unsympathetic teachers—we must marvel at her resiliency. She has never stopped looking for ways to improve her life and the lives of her children. We are so grateful she has shared her story, and believe it will enlighten all who read it.

When I was growing up, I often felt that I was in a magical world that no one else could see, yet I could see people in the world here with me. I never realized that others could not sense things like I did. A more accurate term I could use now is that I never realized that others "perceived" things differently than I did. If I thought something, I believed others could hear those thoughts. I did not begin to learn different until I was much older. I always thought others could hear the sounds I heard, smell things, feel things, just like me. I was not aware that they did not see the wonder, the beauty, the amazing brilliance of light radiating from the trees and plants that I was able to see with ease. I could gaze at the sky for an entire day feeling like I was a part of the sky. The smell of the grass underneath me would bring me a sense of peace.

The entire world amazed me, and the entire world was whereever I was. Nothing else existed. Exploring the world was my favorite thing to do. I wandered very far from home as early as I can recall. The first time I wandered was during my first year of school. I decided to follow a classmate to her home by taking her bus instead of walking with my sister to our home. The challenge was to find my way home after going to a new place. By the age of five, though, I had already explored most of our town and found my way home before too long. My mother went to work when I was four and I was left with my elder siblings, who never noticed I was gone. That was how I was able to get out when ever I wanted, even at night. By nighttime my parents were too tired to notice if I left. Sometimes I would just go and sleep outside. Other times I would wander until I got tired. One of my favorite places to go was in the street, under a certain light, in a certain spot that felt just right. I was rather fortunate to have survived the adventures of my life. My experiences were fun and I learned from them. I learned what not to let children do if I ever became a parent.

I have heard people say that the world is getting worse, that crime and violence is up, and it is not safe in any neighborhood any more. Safety is an illusion. I had heard that it is better to work on feeling brave than it is to work on feeling safe. When I was a child I felt brave, not knowing what safe was, and lacking any real knowledge of the emotion fear when walking into what some might call dangerous or reckless situations.

I felt like I was an adult even when I was a child, only now that I am an adult, I am painfully aware of the fact that I felt like I was an adult because I had no positive adult influences in my life. I had no parental guidance. There were things I knew but I did not know how I knew them, and I did not understand why the adults in my life did not know better than to do what they were doing. It was what I considered simple facts of caring and showing that one cared. I would instead care for the stray animals I found and leave the people alone. I was only six when my sister had her baby. That is when I started learning how to take care of children. It seemed to come naturally for me though, and I began helping with children whenever I could find them around. It also gave me a way to get out of my house. By the time I was twelve, I looked like I was twenty-two. Not many people asked my age and I did not tell.

I knew I wanted to become a parent someday, and I thought it would naturally come in the order that was expected for my generation: marriage, then kids. Teen pregnancy and single parenting was starting to appear more often; young girls that became pregnant were still sent somewhere or forced to give up their babies for adoption, but it was changing. I was aware of the shift only because of the strong emotions involving the debate in our own home. My sister became pregnant when I was five years old, I remember offering to "cut" her baby out for her. My mother was very ashamed of my sister and could not tell our grandmother, her mother. I can still feel the negative way my mother felt during that time. All I could see was the wonder of a new baby.

I was going to do it the right way, marriage first, then children. When I found out that I was pregnant, the reality did not register. I was sixteen and pregnant, and the day I found out I called my mom to tell her, but did not go home for a couple of weeks. My home was my legal address. It was where my parents lived and most of my stuff was, but I was rarely there. Could it be called home then? Home was with anyone I could find to stay with and, looking like a woman, it was rather easy to find someplace to stay.

Looking back is the only way I can really process anything that has happened to me. I have learned that if I stop and turn around I may be able to see the steps it took for me to get to the point I am presently at. It does not always work and sometimes, when I am looking back or talking about the past, people say, "Stop living in the past." I get rather confused with that statement because I am fully aware that I am living in the present— just going back to the past in an attempt to figure things out. More often than not, I can come to a reasonable explanation of how I ended up where I am, and how to avoid doing the same thing again if the outcome was unpleasant. If the outcome was good, I tend to be less able to figure it out. Often people will tell me that what I said was "poetic," or I'll receive a positive response to something I was unaware that I said. How to manage this better is the life challenge I have daily.

Looking back on how I got pregnant was a very long process before I found the answers. Why I got pregnant took even longer. Teenage pregnancy had become an "epidemic" according to some reports. The social stigma and shame was still a fact, as it may still be today. I recently saw a news article about a fourteen-year-old girl getting pregnant and having to go to another state to get married to the father. He was over eighteen. The state officials wanted to have him arrested for statutory rape. That is a term that was impossible to comprehend when I was younger, but now I understand it. I understand the legal term but not the emotional aspect for the legal pursuit in this case. Are the officials trying to "protect" the young girl? If they are, then I think they are too late.

I think I can begin to comprehend the legal case based on my history—based on a situation that occurred in my life. When I think of it that way I wonder if I could support the legal pursuit the state officials were attempting.

Before I turned sixteen years old I became sexually active. Had anyone asked me if I were, I probably would have said no, only because I did not comprehend what the term "sexually active" meant. I now can comprehend the term, but not always the degree of "activity" that accurately defines "sexually active." This topic alone I could discuss for pages, but the point is that I could not have honestly answered yes to that question for a long time. There are also other words adults use to talk about the subject, and I am not exactly sure why they are afraid of talking straight-forwardly about the subject. I now believe that one of my school counselors knew I was sexually active, or at least strongly suspected it. If we could take that same situation now, knowing what we know about autism, the entire situation could have been managed much better. My life as well as many others' lives could have been affected in a more positive manner.

The situation was this. My counselor and I met on a regular basis because I had special needs or problems that had affected my school life for many years. Over the course of time she noticed a change in me that I was not consciously aware of at the time. I am not even sure I would be aware of it so much now, as that is but one of my challenges. I began to dress differently. I am assuming I went from looking like a "good" girl to looking like a "bad" girl. I may never know what she saw different about me because the discussion was never brought up. Instead of talking to me about why I was changing, or even how she saw the changes or what she suspected, she set up an appointment for me and told me where it was and when to be there. I walked to the appointed place, more than ten miles away, and checked in. The place was called "Planned Parenthood," and I had my first female exam in my life. It was degrading and disgusting the way they treated me. I had no time to think about it and had no clue what I was walking into. If I had, then maybe I would have been scared, or not gone at all. I was given a paper bag with enough pills to last several months and told to take one every day at the same time. I know now they were birth control pills.

Looking back at that time in my life, there were many open opportunities for me to learn. There were windows of opportunity to discuss the "facts of life" or the "birds and the bees," but most importantly to discuss with me what they thought I was doing and what I thought I was doing. It was not just my counselor; it was also the institution called "Planned Parenthood." If they knew about autism in girls would they have been able to talk to me differently?

Then of course there is the parental influence. The counselor and the institution told me that they could not and would not discuss my situation with my parents. Not knowing what situation I was in, I never understood these statements. Years later, while I was pregnant, my mother finally said something like, "I really thought you were smart enough not to get pregnant and I know you were on birth control pills." I asked how she knew and it turns out that they filled in the blank check that she gave me to pay the clinic as "Planned Parenthood." Twenty-two years later I found out that my mother got pregnant before she married my dad.

Only now do I see the opportunity we missed. I learned from my history how to discuss the issues of sex with my children, without fear, guilt, or shame. I learned how to be open to the issues and current trends of society in order to help them make their choices; to always continue to grow in my own personal issues on the subject so that I do not push my fears and judgments onto them. I am learning to watch for open windows and doors of opportunities to discuss any topic, especially the most sensitive and important ones. I have learned that I have to be there for them when they need me, not when I can schedule them in.

The summer I got pregnant with my first child is filled with memories that are not easy to explain. Perhaps I do not remember the way most people do, but the memories are still etched in my spirit in a way that will never change. I remember a feeling that I had never had before and felt only one more time after that. I do not seem to recall the dates or times that are based on the machines or units the world uses to measure the quantity of moments; instead I seem to measure based on the quality of those moments. I never wore a watch, and rarely looked at a calendar. Keeping track of what is called a "period" was impossible. The fact that I was taught about menses or that "special time of the month" did not help at all either. I did not know they both referred to the same thing. I actually was not sure what a period was or even the full use of feminine products until after I had the baby, when they taught me in the hospital. I began bleeding heavy when I was eleven and thought I was dying of colon cancer. I had overheard a conversation my dad was having with a relative that had colon cancer, and it was first detected by "bleeding when she went to the bathroom." After I had the baby and figured it out, I decided I would never avoid real talks about this kind of stuff with my children. My first child was a boy, so I thought I would have it easy.

I was still confused, quite literally, as to how I got pregnant. To this day I still believe in divine intervention, even though I also know the physiological aspects now. During the pregnancy I had a shirt made that stated "Kids get in the darndest places." It was a sentiment that was rather funny, and people loved that shirt. I did too, because it explained my confusion without anyone seriously knowing that I was confused. The confusion led to reading as much information as I could get from the doctor. This was the time before the internet. The doctor I had was an amazing person and he seemed to give me extra time to make sure I knew what was going on, as best as he could. He advocated for a natural birth and introduced me to his wife, who was a birth instructor. She ended up being my personal labor coach, too.

By the time I had the baby, the man I had thought was my soul mate was gone, and unable to attend the birth. He and I shared many moments and at times we tried to be more for our baby. The first couple of years he came and went, and then one time was the last time. I heard from a mutual friend he was involved in an accident and did not survive. I may never know the truth, but I knew that people physically disappeared from my life all the time.

The confusion for me at that time in my life was not "why" I got pregnant before I got married, so much as "how." I know that sounds really odd; I have heard people laugh about this topic all the time, yet not many people really know how a pregnancy begins. I let it go once I understood the basics. It was what later led me to the career I chose. I realized I could not change what had happened, and I had a wonderful baby as my miracle. I went on with my life, trying to start all over. Next time, I knew I would do it the right way.

Relationships and dating were never really what I would call difficult. I never understood why people thought it was. I had no problem finding dates or men wanting to date me. The problem was that I had no clue how to really "date." I met a guy and it was immediately all or nothing. Either he was "the one" or he was not. If he was not, I had no reason to even go out on a date with him. If he was then I had no reason to waste time dating, just plan the wedding. That part scared away the good ones, because it was during the time of waiting to set the date that I realized many of the men I thought were "the one" were not even close to it. Of course, those relationships ended before the actual marriage took place. It was an interesting concept for me because I had male friends up until I grew into what looked like a woman. Then the male friends could not do things with me because their girlfriends did not "like" them to be with me. Having male friends became difficult. It literally became impossible for a very long time. Having platonic male friends is something I am only now beginning to enjoy once again.

Having my own child with me was more of a joy than a burden. Of course, I was now living at home, with my parents helping me take care of the baby, and that is why it was relatively easy. He was a colicky baby and I felt it was my fault for not breastfeeding, but the thought of breastfeeding was gross and embarrassing for me. Trying to do it in public was impossible. I tried when I was in the hospital, but was too unsure to really put in the effort. For six months he cried almost constantly, unless he was laying on my belly and chest. He would literally throw up three of every four ounces I fed him. He was losing weight instead of gaining. Love was all I thought I needed to give. I learned that even though breastfeeding may not be the most pleasant thing for me to do it was definitely better for the health of the baby, and I put that piece of knowledge in my library of books in my head labeled "next time."

I was never aware of the developmental milestones and barely managed to get him to the checkups that he needed. I refused to put him in school because I knew he was going to be stuck in it as soon as he turned five and had to go. I was reckless with my own life still. When I left the house, I forgot I had a baby to take care of and went back to the life I knew before, wandering. He was about seven months old when something inside of me clicked. Suddenly I heard him cry; I was not home, but I heard his cry and realized that I was connected to this baby and I had to take care of him. I believe this has something to do with maternal instincts and it helps women on the autism spectrum connect with the world outside ourselves. I have wondered if this is something the males in the spectrum cannot physically experience as easily—the human connection. This topic was the subject of discussion with a male friend of mine on the spectrum. He has no feeling of being connected with anyone or anything on the Earth. It was a conversation we were having specifically about children. He loved children, too, but did not feel connected to them, and imagined if he ever did have any he would still feel the same.

I visualized my life as a helium balloon. I was that big red balloon floating all over the world until my baby was seven months old. That is when my string touched the Earth and I became grounded, with a reason to be a part of this world and the human race. I was almost eighteen as I felt this, and it took almost twenty more years before I could begin to apply it to my life.

Being a woman on the spectrum of autism has alleviated the challenge of finding people to date, but it seems to have increased the possibility of finding what I have recently learned are called "predators." I had come to my own conclusion recently, based on the society I have lived in, that everyone is a trying to sell something to me when they are communicating. They are either trying to get me to buy their product, or buy them, and of course, they want my product for free. This is a cruel opinion, according to some—even harsh in my own opinion, but it is based on the past and not on my present situation. I am looking forward to the next revelation as I venture forward into my life. Until then, the facts of my life lead me to believe this statement. Basically I would buy almost any story. I could always see the potential in any person I met and the good that radiated from them, even if no one else could see it. When I could see it I would invest fully in that person hoping that they would see it, too, and build on it. I would do this without realizing that most people would be able to "see" or "know" what the guy's intentions were.

Adding to this challenge is the fact that I am very disconnected with the emotional and physical aspects of feelings. Meaning that how something feels physically and the emotion I attach to it may not be properly connected. The way I feel things with my senses may not be the same as how the majority of people feel things, but it is definitely like the way other people on the spectrum feel things. I had heard the term "Sensory Integration Dysfunction" (SID) in my attempt to relate to autistic individuals. I could understand why it made sense and may have helped many people begin to understand the differences those of us on the spectrum experience. I personally felt challenged by that concept because it was almost too simple. The way that people "process" things is very complex, and is related to the nervous system and other "systems" that scientists have yet to discover. I had been working on my own "processing" for a very long time, and it was not simple to explain the complex reasons behind why I do things or how I do things; if it were simple I would have already "fixed" it. I had already changed many things, but "fixing" was too complex, since no one knew what needed to be "fixed." I look forward to the day when we will all understand the "difference" even if, by then, many of us have realized that we do not need it to be "fixed."

I can laugh at some of the past situations now and wonder how could I not "see" what I was doing. I also know that I could easily end up doing the same sort of things again because the people, places, or situations always "look" different than the exact situation I was in before. This is also why I sometimes avoid things that might actually be beneficial. Now I guard myself with information and try to have a circle of friends that understand autism or Asperger's, in order to have a protective barrier. There are not enough people that understand it well enough to help us, yet. There are not enough of us that understand it well enough to protect ourselves fully, yet. There are not enough support systems in place, yet. So what has happened to me is still happening to others—on a regular, daily basis. My eldest child is making many of the same mistakes I made because I had not yet learned from my own. He is giving me the opportunity to work with him again, but that does not mean I am prepared enough; just more prepared than before. When my first child turned two years of age, my parents decided to move more than 1300 miles away. I was told that I could come with them if I *really* wanted to. I was also told that they *really* did not have room for me, or enough money to afford a place big enough for my child and me. Once again, another interesting opportunity, and an event in my life that could have gone better, if only we had known more about autism.

I hear professionals say that we need to learn how to "mind-read" and that there are books and computer programs on the subject. Yet I thought I could read minds very well. I could tell by my mother's words and tone of voice that she had no desire to have us move with her. The message was clear that we were not wanted. The message was always "clear" in my mind. I have had these kinds of situations all my life. Because I had many situations like this in my own home, I learned very early to listen to what my mind hears, and not what people are saying. I began gathering evidence to prove my theories and I was always right. My intuition was right: I could read minds. When the "professionals" claimed that people on the spectrum needed to learn to mind-read, I began to doubt that I was on the spectrum. I have come to realize that we need to learn to "face-read," not "mind-read" and that there is another "mind" we are not hearing. Perhaps it is the "conscious" mind of others. However, not too long ago, a friend presented other information to me that made sense, and I am reconsidering my ability to mind-read.

I did not understand what was going on at the time my parents moved. I had depended on them more than I realized. The saying "you don't know what you've got until it's gone" was on my mind while at the same time I had no desire to go with people that I knew did not want us. Many times in my life I have looked back and wondered why my mother said the things she did, or did the things she did. Why did she agree to help me with the baby when I told her I was keeping it? Why did she choose to say yes instead of opening a discussion of what I was going to be faced with? I tried many times as an adult to question her, to find out what her motives were. What was she thinking and doing? Each time I did anything to try to improve our relationship it only made it worse. Just over a year after their move, my father died suddenly. Another person had disappeared from my life, and that is why I married my first husband.

This time I was doing it right, I thought. I was married and got pregnant several months later. I would have really benefited from having a mentor in my life who would ask me the questions that I did not know how to ask myself: Why? What? Now that we are beginning to learn more about autism/Asperger's I hope that things will change for the better for all of us. I hope that things will change enough so that my life can be an inspiration, not something to fear. That the experiences I have had will help others understand why they need to acknowledge that girls, too, have autism/Asperger's. It may not fit the classic definition but we do share three common traits with everyone else on the spectrum: language challenges, social challenges, idiosyncrasies (such as obsessions or compulsions). After receiving my diagnosis, many images and episodes in my life began flooding back in my mind, as if they were demanding to be properly filed. One such memory was of a time when I was in my special school. Several of the teachers would tell me that I had to say something more than "hello," which is all I knew how to say when I saw someone I liked (which was only a few of the teachers). They recognized a social problem but did not recognize what to do about it or what the real problem was.

The woman that helped me to come to terms with my diagnosis pointed out how a simple act by a "pretty young woman" toward a man with "impure" intentions would naturally lead to the situations I found myself in. The reality is that many of us are still going through the same challenges. We often get through life by maintaining a facade of what people call "normal" and we do have some successful moments. Inside, we are dying to get out, but have no clue how. We instead find joy in pure solitude, sometimes to the point of complete withdrawal from the world. When that happens no one understands why or how to get us back, least of all ourselves. Sometimes the very people we love the most are the ones causing the problems because they do not understand the logic of our thinking. The key that opened doors for me was the correct and accurate diagnosis that I have Autism Spectrum Disorder.

Some women are subjected to more abusive relationships than I was, which makes it hard for them to get out alive. Some of the women end up in prisons, or shelters, or homeless. Some end up in the mental health system labeled as "mentally ill." Every time I was at the point of withdrawal and in need of complete solitude, those around me could not comprehend my need, so they could not support it. Instead, they made it worse. Services under the heading of any mental diagnosis made it worse. I would take their diagnosis and work with it, but it never made sense and it never made a difference. I recall happily announcing that I had depression to a few friends and they all just looked at me with total disbelief. I can understand why. I was always cheerful, happy, and what some called vivacious. Of course then when I tried to explain this to a psychiatrist I was told I must be bi-polar. I was extremely frustrated but worked with that one for a while too. It did not fit. Of course being a "mental" patient I had no authority to make rational or logical decisions because of my own "illness." The system that was set up to help me was, in fact, making me worse. I am sure it was not their intent; they just did not know how and still do not.

I was only 20 years old and happy to be having another baby, my baby girl this time. It seemed logical to me that I would have a girl. I already had my boy, so of course it would be a girl. What I could not understand was why I was so extremely irritable and short tempered with everyone around me. I did not recognize that my son was having challenges in areas that might have been picked up by what we now call early intervention. I worked evening shifts so I would have to leave him with anyone I could find. I had no reason to enforce a bedtime, and didn't have any under-standing why it was needed. There were no set rules and we ate when we wanted and what we felt like eating. Standards of nutrition were beyond my ability to comprehend. As long as there was food, I thought I was doing fine. Only during my pregnancy did I even think about eating well and I did take a vitamin. I also quit smoking for the babies. I went back to it after having them. As they got older and I learned more, I would choose to not smoke in the house. I realize that part of this was due to the messages society was sending us. My father had cancer and smoking was beginning to get the blame. I still had to go back and forth several times before realizing how bad it made me feel. Work relationships became impossible while I was pregnant, and I thought it was related to my preg-nancy. I had no reason to think I was unhappy. Another example of my inability to connect how I was feeling emotionally and physically with the situation and circumstances I was in. Now I can understand because I am not in it. I was divorced and raising my two children before my baby girl was four years old.

It was during that time that I almost began to understand what I was doing to them. I began to understand that they needed more than I could give them, so I went back to school and became a Registered Nurse with the intent of becoming a midwife. The miracle of each child's conception and birth is what led me to this career choice. The caring and compassion of the first doctor and his wife led me to want to be around people like that and become a person like that. I had no one helping me with career choices; there were no services that could help me to understand or decide what I needed to do in life or why I was making the choices I was making, no one to help me understand myself. My logical side knew I now needed to be a provider, but the curious side wanted to learn about the body and birth, and to be the kind of mentor others were to me. Not realizing how difficult social relationships were, I was setting myself up for failure from the beginning. Not realizing how certain environments affected me physically was also going to lead to problems I was unable to plan for.

It was during that time in my life that I began to feel completely lost as to what I really wanted and needed in life. I wanted to be a wife and mom but relationships, I finally began to admit, were impossible for me to figure out. I gave up on that plan.

Working on a career was much easier compared to working on relationships. There were steps, routes, degrees, and road maps to where I wanted to go. The road maps were then written out for me and I began running on those paths.

In one way, I was gaining confidence and what some might call self-esteem. I was beginning to learn about other cultures and other worlds that I had not known existed. I began to open up academically and wonder why grade school and high school had not been as interesting. On the other hand, I was failing at the one thing I thought I knew how to do naturally: mothering.

It was at this time in my life I had the opportunity to meet other teenage girls who had given their babies up for adoption. I recall how angry I used to get when my friends who had babies around the same time as I did, gave their babies up. This was different, though. The girls I met were not the same; somehow they were different than the girls I had known. They seemed to have come to terms with their decision because of the child, and not because of their own feelings. This was a concept I had never thought of. It was about their choice to give their child a better life than what they had to offer it. It was not only about age, or they that were going to lose their freedom, it was about college funds, two parents, and a home that they could not provide. My life was changed forever by their stories. For the first time ever I began to be able to comprehend there was perhaps another perspective than my own. It has been more than fifteen years since then and I am just beginning to realize there is always a different perspective than my own—a perspective that I cannot imagine but have so much fun trying to discover, when I have the energy. People are like puzzles to me, that is the fun part. It is also the part that leaves me baffled because I am unable to put together my own puzzle, called "my life." One situation can haunt my mind for hours and days, and linger on for months before I can come to a satisfactory solution and am able to move on. Sometime I have to put it in a room in my mind similar to unsolved mysteries. One day I may get the right clue, evidence, or material, to help me figure it out. During this time of my life, a single mom of two wonderful children, I put the file called "marriage" or "relationships" in that room and worked on my career.

For the first time ever my children had to have a bedtime, because I had to get homework done in the evening and was only able to do so if they were sleeping. I was truly amazed at the difference in their academic work and some of the behaviors at school. My son was the one with challenges and problems with his "behavior" that I never understood. I had no problems with his behavior. The fact that I had no expectations may have been part of the reason. At the time I thought it was the teachers because he would have a good year, then a bad year, followed by another bad or good year. He received special education for a short time but his grades were good when he had a good year. He was diagnosed with ADD/ADHD according to the school and we tried medication. It made him different but did not help at all. The teacher for that year must have been a different kind of teacher, because she admitted that based on her experience, it was not ADD/ADHD. She had her own children and several students with ADD/ADHD. If my son had it, then she would have seen the difference with the medications. She could not tell me what other options I had or what else it might possibly be. Knowing there was nothing "wrong" with my child, other than school, I was not serious about looking for help. I was never his advocate. I did not know how to be.

Even though I had given up on relationships, they did not give up on me. I met and married my second husband through a series of events that I could not have predicted or planned, and another miracle entered my life. He was my hero, my knight in shining armor, he came to save me. Our dreams were similar, and he knew how to obtain them. Soon we had our first child, my third, and another boy. From the very beginning, this pregnancy was different. The doctors were questioning the functioning of my thyroid because of physical ailments that started before the pregnancy. I was in my late twenties and thought I was just getting too old to have children. My heart would race for no reason, I felt like throwing up almost always. When the pregnancy was found, they dismissed these as conditions related to the pregnancy. I needed to sleep always. Fatigue took over my life and I was barely making it through the days. The day the baby was born, I woke up, and was overjoyed with all that I had.

Each day afterward was filled with constant confusion. The baby had more energy than anyone else in the house, needing less sleep than any of us, and wearing on everyone's nerves. I was confused with the way my husband treated my other children; he was always teasing them. My daughter learned quickly to tease back, have a tougher side, and not to let whatever he said affect her, but my son could only pretend. Perhaps that was the hardest part for me. I was constantly told this was "the way" men do things but it never felt right to me. I never really understood the act of teasing if it hurt someone.

The teasing spread to include everything my son did; he could do nothing right, and every time he made a mistake, I would of course reprimand him. He would lose privileges and his allowance until he wasn't able to do things or go places. Finally, after our second baby was born, my fourth child, I took time off work to help all of them and the solution for him came to us in the form of mentors from a local church. A youth pastor volunteered to be his what I now call "faith brother." Soon my son had several adults in his life and he began to flourish as long as he was not at home.

Working on my career was still relatively easier, more structured, and a part of me wanted to focus only on that aspect of my life. The demands of a house, four kids, and a husband made it almost impossible to do it as well as I wanted to, as well as I knew I could. For a short time I was able to maintain a balance, but right before my fourth child was born, the third one began having medical problems, seizures, infections, illness, constant runny nose, and keeping a babysitter was a serious problem. I had to change my schedule and positions more than once in order to be available to my family and take care of the child no one would watch. Reminders of the problems I had with my first were beginning to haunt me, but the connection was still not made. He was placed into a preschool because he had "developmental disabilities" but that was all that it was called. I was not connecting the proverbial "dots"; I was not realizing how the medical conditions and the reasons for the problems with babysitters and pre-school could be connected. I recall that time very well. The teachers had a look on their face, a look that I had seen only on the faces of doctors before that day. It was the look on the doctor's face as he or she told the family or loved one that the patient did not make it. A polite way of say-ing the person was dead. I never understood why they did not just come out and say the word "dead." I did not understand what the teachers were saying either. I heard the words: "lacks appropriate social skills, inappro-priate communication skills, and major deficits in fine and gross motor skills." I was so upset and I just assumed that they wanted my child on drugs, so I stated the fact and left, upset. Anger was the only emotion that I knew when I felt that way. Now I see how another window was opened, a window to growth and understanding if I had only understood what they were trying to tell me. If they had only known how to manage an adult and child on a spectrum called Autism.

Cody, my third child, was different in ways I did not comprehend. I knew it was hard to take care of him and I knew I could not explain it. Larger day care settings were too much for him and smaller homes or private day care were better for him—but harder on the person providing the care. It is easier now to understand how and why things were harder with my son. Autism explains it. It is that simple for me now, but not as simple for others to understand yet. I hope to be able to help others understand the complexities of autism.

Some of the challenges we had with Cody started early, when he was younger than three years old, and some were present from the beginning. His inability to sleep was noticeable, but we thought it to be just the way he was. I now know he has sleep apnea, after having a sleep study done.

The physical aspects of his nasal passageway and airway are not the same size as most people's his age. Looking at him from the front, he looks to have an overbite; looking at him from the side view, his lower chin seems to be set in much farther. Does this mean there are physical abnormalities causing him difficulty with breathing? This is something we are just now investigating.

He walked with a bounce and on the tips of his toes. Later he was recognized as having decreased responses, sometimes absent reflexes in the lower extremities. The reasons were not addressed by the medical professionals. His odd walk led to him having difficulty running. He slowed down his activity as he got older and before long had no desire to play outside with other kids. He had a runny nose all the time, later to be diagnosed as "environmental allergies," with treatments that barely made a difference. Once he was diagnosed with asthma and after being medicated for months, we found out it was not asthma just an asthmatic-like episode. Together these contributed to increased weight and decreased activity.

I was told by the preschool that he had gross- and fine-motor coordination deficiency, and that they would work on these issues. How it impacted his life out of school I was unaware of. How or why to treat him out of school was beyond my comprehension. The fact that he could not ride a bike was covered up by the fact that he did not want to even try.

Playing in the pool was the only exercise he could or would participate in. I signed him up for baseball one year, but he never understood the concept. Also, he was afraid the ball was going to hit him when it was thrown near him, causing him to duck or move aside instead of hitting it with the bat or try to catch it when in the field. While many children at the age of five may not be that interested in learning to play baseball, and while in the field may not be able to stay still or pay attention to the game, Cody's inability went much farther than average, and many times we could only laugh. He would be in his own world, bouncing around in his space, oblivious to anyone watching. Once the ball rolled into his space and he spotted it, he picked it up and proudly lifted his treasure to the sky, never throwing it to anyone because he was so happy he found it and had it he did not want to let it go. At the time it was just funny, but now I see it as another lost opportunity to learn.

He played with small cars. He would line them all up in a row. Never did I wonder why. He preferred to climb into tight spaces, like the kitchen cabinets, and stay in there. He had problems with going to sleep and had what some would call night terrors.

Toilet training was a personal issue for me, I hated diapers, but trying to push him seemed to make it worse. When he was around four, delayed in my opinion, but maybe not a serious delay according to the professionals, I realized that the best way to toilet-train him was to bring the toilet into the only room he would sit still in, the living room. I recall people; other parents especially, telling me that it was an inappropriate way to teach, because the toilet was in the bathroom. That training him to use the toilet in a room it was not in would never work. Somehow their logic made sense to them, and mine made sense to us. It worked. The only way he would sit still long enough, to relax enough, to be able to let it out, was in front of the television with his favorite movie on.

He had a hard time at school, and though the teachers would tell me the issues, how he could not play the way other children his age do, they never told me how it was different. I could not see it either because I had nothing to compare it to. When they pointed out that he would "refer to himself in third person," I did not understand what that meant. When they explained he refers to himself by name, instead of "me" or "I," I still did not understand why it was a problem until I understood the diagnosis of Autism.

I have heard stories that some children regress, or lose skills that they had before the diagnosis. I have heard that these regressions are what lead many parents to find out what is wrong and that is when they get the diagnosis. The fact that I did not notice the regressions that were present (he stopped speaking for a few months) until after they returned, may have been part of the reason he (and his younger brother) were not diagnosed earlier. He was in speech, and therapy at school (both were in early treatment for aspects of autism without the name put on them). When he came home he was not in any treatment; he was allowed to be a kid. Unlike many parents, I encouraged their needs more than my own. They were kids that needed to play and explore their world; our home was their world. I could not keep it show-room presentable and I came to terms with that for them. The house was always kid friendly and kid proof with the most dangerous of things not even in the house.

I learned early on that it did no one any good to take them with me on errands, like to the grocery store or department stores. I did those errands when I could leave them with their father or someone else. Now I will take one or both only when I have the energy and do not "need" to get it done, so I can teach them what we are doing. I also learned early that typical family activities were not for our family. I was fortunate enough to have a career that allowed me to work other than a typical workweek or day.

They had issues at school and we had a great school system that recognized their needs and helped them to achieve academically in spite of the challenges and without a formal diagnosis of any kind. They helped the best they could. Cody was doing great academically but was unable to function socially. For some reason, no one was worried about it. His brother was still in preschool but they took a special interest in his needs and enjoyed meeting them, even when his behavior was "inappropriate."

The extra energy it took to keep the children from becoming out of control around others, like at school, wore on my physical health. I was falling ill to every infection that came my way. I was losing time from work and using up all my vacation and sick time. When the final straw hit, in 2002, I had no reserves. Suddenly, and without warning of any kind, my husband, at the age of thirty-eight, died of a heart attack driving to work. When I got the news, my professional mode kicked in, but so did my lack of social understanding. I was not at all sensitive to the potential pain my children would feel, I had no clue how they would react, I had no resources to draw on other than my own experience, personal and professional, and the need for straightforward, honest facts was all I knew. When I told them, their reaction hurt more than the news of his death. The pain is still present when I write this. Could I have handled this better?

The entire process was a fog. The youngest one, always accused of being oversensitive, would not stop crying. The older one, always accused of being a little "slow," had no reaction. One would not go near the casket; the other would not go away. My eldest would not even attend the funeral. My daughter tried to help. Life held too many changes at that time. We moved to a less expensive place not realizing the effect the school system would have on them. I tried to continue work and school and all the routines we had, but my boys began having fears beyond the comprehension of most, and I was the only one that could help. I was the only one that understood their pain without any words—words that none of us could find.

I put my career on hold in order to finally figure out what the physical aspect of all our challenges were, why others did not understand us, and what to do about it. Autism diagnosis explains it very well, but even I was not putting the pieces of the puzzle together.

I had never really heard of autism, not even in nursing school, that I was consciously aware of—meaning it was one of those things that I may have heard but it did not register in my mind because it had been put in that file "to figure out later." The reason I suspect that it had been spoken around me is because when I was introduced to the term, I had to know what it was. Perhaps my need to know was because of the relevance it actually had to my life. It was about a year before the death of my husband. A friend of mine had an autistic child that I never met, though I had heard about some of the problems. For some reason I needed to investigate. The overwhelming amount of information, the confusion with technical data and debates was not helping. My friend gave me the book by Thomas McKean, *Soon Will Come the Light,* and I immediately felt a connection but did not understand it. I found Thomas and began a friendship with him over the internet. Our life paths were very similar and we were both even living in the state of Virginia at that time.

During the time of our friendship I began to understand Thomas and aspects of autism, but not what the "problem" was or why it was tagged a "devastating disorder," or why parents were sometimes angry and mean when it came to talking about their child with autism. Where was the pain and anger coming from? I did not understand

Looking back to my time with Thomas, before receiving our diagnosis, I remember a moment that could now be laughed at under the heading of "an autistic conversation." Part of the reason I was confused about autism is that some of the common "behaviors" that were written about in the research were present in my son Cody. He was now nine years old, though. The behavior that was once his bounce and tip-toe walk was now a walk and rock with arms flapping. In school he was observed as "rocking in his seat" and "flapping his arms" on a regular basis. So I asked Thomas, seriously, if he (the "expert" on autism, according to the sticker on his book) thought Cody could have autism. Thomas did a very funny thing: first he asked how old Cody was, and after I told him, he stopped walking, changed the way he stood to straight up, his head became straight forward and up taller, and his voice changed as he stated, "It is formally diagnosed between the years of three and five. Cody is nine so he cannot be." The question was answered and the topic was over. He went back to the way he had walked before and there was no further discussion. Now I realize how both of our communication challenges contributed to that, but at the time it occurred, I dismissed the possibility immediately.

Thomas has an amazing community of supporters that is helping him with issues of life that he could not handle on his own. I was welcomed into that community and they were there for us all after the death occurred, I will forever be thankful for his and their friendship. It was his friendship and the things he did around me and to me that made me begin to understand some of the things I had done "wrong" in relationships. I still had not put the puzzle together or understood the connection between autism and our family. It was coming together, though. The bridge connecting the two worlds was only a few bricks away from completion.

Looking for answers to understand autism, the physical challenges we all had, the emotionally charged circumstances and lack of social support, I turned to faith and was given a mentor and guide in the form of another new friend.

I found a retired physician located in the UK that had personal and professional connections with Dr. Lorna Wing. He was willing to discuss with me every issue that I needed to talk about, and after many months he guided the physicians working with me on aspects of my health. I know that his input saved my life more than once. The amazing details of that relationship cannot be easily described. The miracles would make a wonderful movie, but for now I will just tell part of what came out of it.

When my friend was not available to me his mother would fill in. She was an amazing woman that had already raised her children, one with serious health issues, including autism and a rare form of asthma. It was at that time that my son was diagnosed with asthma. She thought it sounded odd and instructed me as to how to treat it and how to record findings to bring back to the doctor. These findings led to the removal of his diagnosis and the many medications he was on. She also informed her son, the doctor, of what had happened in his absence. Having practiced with pediatrics, he asked for a full medical history of my son and then left full instructions for a physical exam to be done. The results of the exam were given to him and he returned with a profile of my son, including details that I had never mentioned, including the rocking, flapping, and the severe scream- ing when his head was touched, and the final verdict was "autism." The case almost exactly described what Leo Kanner had described, according to my friend. The light went on!

It made so much sense that I was happy to finally know the truth! I called a meeting at the school and went to tell them the great news, only to begin another journey I did not comprehend: the legal and business workings of the school system (which even led them to call the social system to eval- uate if I was a danger to my children). A similar story made headlines shortly after my challenge, and was discussed among other adults on the spectrum. A mother had lost her child because the diagnosis of autism had not been understood. That is another story for another time as well; for now let me explain how it helped us as a family.

I am not exactly sure why doctors have a hard time giving the diagnosis of autism. I may never really know, but I did meet some doctors who believed that autistic people could not talk. If a doctor believes that all people with autism cannot talk, they will ask if the child talks, or if they hear the child talk while in the office they dismiss the possibility of autism. If they understand it is a problem with communication instead of verbal talking alone they may look deeper.

I understood that the term autism and Asperger's were often used to describe the same thing. I began to realize that there could be many other terms used to describe the spectrum of autism including the term PDD- NOS. I knew one mother that had a child with the diagnosis of

"Asperger's," so I told her that my son was diagnosed with "Autism." She immediately stated "well, you have it a lot worse than us then, because we only have Asperger's." Every different professional we went to there gave it a different name, but none of them explained a reason for the different diagnosis. I finally found the one professional in our area that gave me the statistical data on a report done by Harvard and Yale that the consistency of accurate diagnosis between professionals was less than 35%, and because of that he referred to it as "Autism Spectrum," plain and simple. The doctor from the UK had told me that it is not appropriate to label them specifically until they are adults when the functional level of competency in basic life skills could be determined. Instead, we need to work on helping them improve their skills now. We began working with this doctor only.

I also understood that it was a neurological difference that they had, even if there was no medical evidence to support the fact yet. I knew every behavior had a logical reason to it. While the school attempted to gather evidence and data to prove my child was an "emotionally disturbed behavior problem" that needed more discipline, I set out to gather data to prove he was not. I took classes on business, health, education, and communication, in ways that were not mainstream. I worked with my son, walked with him to observe his issues, began showing up at school without notice to see what was going on and every time they called me in with another complaint I was armed with the knowledge that he was in fact on the autism spectrum, and was not "choosing" to be defiant. It took the entire year, but in the end the system changed, and Cody (and our family) is now considered a pioneer by some of those that worked directly with him, as well as by the people responsible for making changes in the system. I would like to share some of the stories as examples.

First it started at home. I had to slow down and watch him to see what was going on. He still has not figured out one of my favorite stories. I am beginning to understand the humor aspect of autism stories that at one time I did not like too much. If this one is not funny I apologize; I thought it was.

One day we were running late for an appointment. Running late put pressure on my children and I knew that long ago and had learned to compensate by always giving more time than we needed, but this time I was behind. Slipping back into the mode I was in before, I demanded that he hurry up! "Throw on your shoes and socks now, we got to go!" I demanded as I ran up the stairs to get ready. I came back down several minutes later, which was more than enough time for him to have accomplished the task, so when I saw him laughing and playing with his sock I almost screamed. Instead, I covered my mouth and stopped to watch him. This time I saw the open window of opportunity and looked inside. Between his giggles he finally noticed that I was standing there, and in all serious-ness he looked at his feet and then at me and stated: "Mom, you are silly." I was too angry and stressed to reply so I just stood there and that gave him the time to tell me why. "Mom, you cannot throw socks on!" and gig-gled even more. I asked him to pick up his shoes and socks to put on in the car. (another issue since he hated walking barefoot but he was still laughing about my incompetence and was able to comply). Once we were on the road and I was calmer, I asked him what he thought I meant. He really thought there might have been a "teleporter" or some device or a special way to actually "throw" your socks on. He realized after many attempts that I must in fact be the silly one, as he spent all that time and many different ways to try it with no success. I realized then that after the diagnosis, I was able to look at his actions in a way that was different from how I had perceived them before.

One of the next things that I realized was the fact that people on the spec-trum can "forget" things that seem unforgettable. For instance, they would forget who their own parents were if away from them. This explains now why the fears about me leaving never really went away, and became worse after traumatic events (like the death). Cody had been treated for asthma because of breathing problems and often had upset stomachs. Watching him closely, I noticed he never blew his nose. I had taught him how but I had to teach him again every day for months. Now I do not have to do this as much, but sometimes I do still have to remind him to blow his nose. If I do not, he regresses back to what he did when he was younger, sniffle it back up, and then he gets worse infections and sick to his stom-ach, or it is all over his shirt as he uses that to wipe it off. The nausea, throwing up, and dizziness were being attributed to his "emotional issues that I was not addressing" and he needed counseling according to the school. Learning to blow his nose began to alleviate some of the problems.

Food was the next one. I had heard there were several diets that parents had claimed cured their child. We looked into some of them and even did one for a short time. The reality was that they were too "restrictive," a term I learned in the legal school system. The diets would have to be maintained constantly and any little "cheating" would cause months of setback. I could not see how that would really help in his case, so we approached one at a time. Soon we found several items that, if he ate too much of or any at all, made him feel sick the next day. I helped him to connect the dots so he would understand why should choose not to eat the food. I even allowed him to eat it in excess, if he really thought he wanted it. He soon began to learn what not to eat, and to eat other things in moderation.

I would walk to school with him to find more information. I had learned from my own challenges that connecting the physical and emotional aspects of things was almost impossible. It was something we all needed help with. From walking with Cody I learned a lot.

I have a picture of my boys from the first day of kindergarten for the youngest one. We lived across the street, so they had a very short walk. I took the picture of Cody putting his arm around his brother as they walked. It is one I still adore and have on my desk. I did not know how autism fit into our life that day, so I thought that Cody was taking care of his little brother by having his arm around him and keeping him close. As the days went on, though, his brother became annoyed and did not want Cody to hold onto him. This issue became one of the "behavior problems" at school. When I started walking with him, I began to see that Cody needed something or someone to hold onto. About halfway to school he would turn pale, stop walking, sometimes stumble a little, then "space out" for a few seconds. After such an episode he would complain of being tired, thirsty, and confused. I began giving him water to take to school and sometimes carried his bag for him. Remarks by the teachers were rude and hurtful. I thought the kids were supposed to be the "bullies" but the teachers were the ones making remarks to us like "your mother shouldn't be carrying your bag; you're old enough to do it yourself." I had to explain to them that he had health issues that made it difficult. Some would apologize but others made jokes about it and how to put something like that in an IEP. If I heard these things, I am sure he did, too.

Once I reported these symptoms to the neurologist, tests were done that showed that they were a form of mild seizures. Medication was not needed, but helping Cody to understand, and teaching others to watch for them, was. They also looked like they could be a "panic attacks" so I taught him how to recognize the feelings and not panic. Getting him away from cruel teachers was also a priority. The students actually helped Cody and liked him.

My friend Thomas helped me understand an aspect of autism that I have not seen reported much. There is a system of our body that is responsible for telling our brain and body where we are in relationship to the world and surroundings. From watching Cody, I am thinking that perhaps he has this problem but is not able to verbalize it for many reasons. Among these reasons I am sure is the same reason that I was never aware of anything really being wrong with me. I have lived in this body all my life, and it is the only one I know. I did not know I needed glasses until people around me noticed I was squinting. I did not know I could see better until I had been given glasses. Cody, as well everyone else on the spectrum, is dealing with things he does not perceive as being different or wrong. He looks down when he walks, always. The school said it was a sign of his "emotional issues." Later I understood that this is something "depressed" people do. Cody is always watching his feet as he walks, because he stumbles and trips very easily. Now I have finally found a person that understands how occupational therapy can help and will start working with him. School, on the other hand, only offered occupational therapy related to schoolwork. Some schools still may not understand the other aspect of this therapy. I wonder if the "self stim" behavior, as it is often called, of rocking, helps them to feel where they are?

As I was working on understanding the physical aspects, I know that understanding the emotional aspects were important as well. But I had to address the complaints the teachers had. I was working on some alternative avenues to help Cody study for tests, knowing that he did well with testing. Modifications that were already in place for him were effective, and I knew his scores would help me prove he was not "stupid" (as they would imply by joking about his odd behaviors and failing grades).

The first issue was actually very difficult for me because I did not understand it well enough myself. When I found the person to test my son I was truly blessed. After testing Cody for several hours, and watching him closely, he found some interesting things. The most interesting was related to Cody's inability to write correctly. It is a problem called "dysgraphia."

We knew he had sloppy handwriting, but the end product was all they ever looked at. Cody could occasionally produce a rather neat handwritten project. Because of this fact, the school used it as "proof" that he was capable of such work. What they did not know is how much time it took him, or what the task involved: was it a written copy of something or was it something he had to write while listening? It also proved that he could "print" neatly but he was now expected to be using "cursive" and the only thing he could manage to write in cursive was his own name. Until he was watched during the actual process of writing no one knew he was writing most things the opposite way than he should have been taught. We are taught to start a "C" from the top and curve down; he would start from the bottom and curve up. He did this with all letters. This is why he could never transition into cursive. This discovery alone explained why he could not physically write cursive, and his problems with processing explained why he could not write while listening. His grades were failing because he was marked off for printing or not taking notes in class during lecture. This was a skill they demanded he learn because it is expected and a "skill he will need in college and high school." More than once I had to explain to them, even after having it documented by two professionals, that it was equal to taking a wheelchair away from a child that uses one and expecting that child to walk to the bathroom. His grades did not improve, the teacher refused to change her decision and while she was filling out the forms to hold him back a year, the standard tests came back with scores above average. The officials overseeing our case could not support her decision. My poor social skills were obvious during that time.

Another day I was called in because they were going to suspend him for "refusing to do an assignment." When I got there, everyone—the teacher, the principal, and the office staff—was already talking to him about his "behavior." He was already beyond upset and withdrawn. I decided to ask the teacher to tell me her side. She was happy to offer "proof" that he was refusing and being defiant. Her evidence again proved my point: he has autism. She stated that all the children had to write a paragraph describing themselves and Cody refused to do it. We had already had several debates regarding all writing projects, and we knew that, because of his handwriting, all writing projects were going to be a challenge. But they had not accepted that aspect when this happened. She went on to tell me the entire story, and how Cody just sat there pouting and refusing to do it. She knew he could do it and tried to convince him to do it, but he still refused. Once the class was finished, she kept him after because he had "refused" to do the paragraph. It was after all the other children left that she pulled out a mirror and sat down next to him. She put the mirror in front of him and pointed to his face, the color of his eyes, the color of his hair, and the color of his glasses. Then, in less than five minutes, he had the paragraph done. Her point was that he could write the paragraph, and since he had done it with her help after class, she thought it proved her point. I was having a hard time understanding her point and how her story "proved" it, and I am sure Cody was just as confused. She felt this justified with her decision to give him a punishment, and she wanted my approval and support. I refused. Now I understood how the language problems alone can cause challenges, I also understood what other teachers had told me about "referring to himself in third person," and that it was a great challenge for him to understand the concept of "me" or "self." So of course a project like "describe yourself" would cause confusion for him, because he did not know what his "self" looked like until she brought the mirror over and pointed it out to him. Cody was correct; he could not do it. But he also could not explain why, and that is why he began saying "I cannot do it" and they began to hear "I will not do it." She did admit that he had said at first he could not do it. Once he was pushed, he may have begun to act or behave worse. Wouldn't anyone in that situation?

Each time I stood up for him, each time I explained the reasons for his behavior, Cody came out of his shell a little, out of the world that he had withdrawn into. I began giving him books about autism and Asperger's, so he would know that he was not the only one. This is when I started to see how my eldest son became so lost. I stood up for him but not as well as I do for my children now. I am becoming educated and staying involved, working with the school system, not against it, to make a difference for my children, and every child after them, in a positive way. I would have never been able to do what I am doing for them now if I had not already had one child pushed through the system. Every day I see the future for my boys. I see it in my life and in the life of their eldest brother. I see it because we lived it and are living it. What I do not know is how to get us to the other side.

If you focus on what is wrong with your child, that is all you will see. If you believe this is a devastating disorder that needs a cure, then your child will feel the negativity around him even if he does not understand why. If you limit children with negativity or box them into a category, they cannot grow.

If you focus only on what is right with them you will only see that aspect. A parent in denial will not help anyone.

But if you use the diagnosis as a key that opens the door to understanding, the entire world will change for the better. Accept your child's uniqueness, embrace her need for help. Find out how by approaching each physical, social, and emotional challenge for each individual and helping them overcome it.

Those of you who just "know" this social stuff naturally, please help us by slowing down and thinking about all the steps you know "naturally." We need to learn them.

To those on the spectrum: we need you also to teach, learn, and help each other and our younger generation.

For Me,
a Good Career
Gave Life Meaning

Meet Temple Grandin, Ph.D.

D r. Grandin is one of the most respected individuals with high-functioning autism in the world. She presents at conferences nationwide, helping thousands of parents and professionals understand how to help individuals with autism, Asperger's Syndrome, and PDD. She has authored *Emergence: Labeled Autistic, Thinking in Pictures, Animals in Translation* (which spent many weeks on *The New York Times'* Best-Seller List), and her most recent work, *Unwritten Rules of Social*

Relationships, co-authored with Sean Barron. She also designs livestock-handling systems, improving the treatment of cattle and other animals all over the world.

Dr. Grandin doesn't claim to speak for all women on the spectrum, but many will agree when she says that "emotional relatedness is not the major motivator in the lives of a certain subset of individuals with Asperger's or high-functioning autism."

Like many people on the autism spectrum, she has found her life's satisfaction in her work. She has chosen celibacy because it eliminates the complicated problem of having to unearth the land mines buried in the social landscape (a problem shared by most people on the spectrum). Other people may make different choices—but Temple's story should caution us all against automatically conforming to society's relationship standards.

I was asked to explain in this paper why I was never interested in dating. During my teenage years I never became boy crazy. My good friend Carol swooned over the Beatles and howled with delight when the Beatles appeared on the *Ed Sullivan Show*. I thought they were cute, but I did not have the emotional reaction that the other girls had. They were experiencing something that I did not experience.

At my boarding school, the big concern was making sure that none of the girls ran off in the bushes with a guy. I observed that certain rules were much more important than other rules. Students got in a lot of trouble for smoking and wandering off in the woods with a boy without a chaperone. From my observations, I figured out that if I could be absolutely trusted not to have sex, I would be able to get many extra unofficial privileges. It was at this time that I developed my rule classification system. The four types of rules are:

- Really Bad Things—murder, arson, theft
- Courtesy Rules—table manners, saying please
- Illegal, but not bad—flying my kite without a chaperone

- Sins of the System—sex, smoking, and drinking were the sins of the system for my boarding school.

Smoking and sex were sins of the system that had severe penalties. By carefully testing the limits I figured out that I could get away with many small infractions such as staying up past 10:00 p.m. and flying my kite without a staff member because I could be trusted absolutely to not smoke or have sex. Basically I gave up activities that many people consider central to life so I could do things I found more interesting. Being allowed to watch a science fiction movie past the normal 10:00 p.m. bedtime was more important than dating. I just did not care about the girlfriend/boyfriend-type relationship.

I did have friends but the relationships were through shared interests. In high school it was horses and later in life it was friends in the construction industry. We had a good time because we built things together.

For me the most fun thing to talk about was how to build things. During my formative years I also saw a lot of marital strife. I never saw a marriage that I could picture myself being happy in. There was no satisfactory model for me to use as a template.

Career Makes Life Worthwhile

In college and later in life, I was happiest when I was doing projects. Mr. Carlock, my science teacher, challenged my mind with interesting projects. As a young adult, some of the happiest days of my life were working in equipment design where I had to figure out how to design things. Using my mind to create equipment that improved how the cattle were treated gave my life meaning.

Unlike most people, I am what I do rather than how I feel. This is a hard concept for many people to understand. Educational professionals and psychologists who have no contact with the technical industries find this hard to understand. In my work with the meat industry I know other people similar to me who live for either their career or their hobby. I had a good discussion with a lady in the computer industry about her successful marriage via shared interests. She met her husband at a science fiction convention and they liked each other because they both loved to talk about computer technology. She described romantic, candle-lit dinners, where they were so happy spending four hours discussing computer data storage systems. Their relationship was all about intellectual interests and not about feelings.

I am very concerned that many parents and professionals fail to understand that emotional relatedness is not the major motivator of the lives of a certain subset of individuals with Asperger's or high functioning autism. They try to make us into something that we are not. I can learn social skills, and learning social skills is very important, but I can not learn emotional relatedness. They need to understand that having meaningful work is what gives life meaning. I have read and heard about some sad cases where teachers and parents were so concerned about the fact that a teenager did not care about marriage that they failed to develop the child's intellectual life. One parent wanted to take her child out of computer science class to make him more social. The irony is that computer science class was probably the one place her child had friends and a social life. I told her that depriving the child of computer science class would be really bad.

Wide Variation

I have been reasonably happy even though I am totally celibate. Celibacy avoided a lot of complicated social situations. Sometimes I realize I am missing experiences that other people have, but I keep myself super busy doing many interesting things. My lifestyle is not for everyone with Asperger's. It was easier for me because the brain circuits that made my friend Carol swoon over the Beatles are just not hooked up in me. Others on the spectrum want to get married and be emotionally related. It all depends which circuits get connected.